Remembering Vonda

1948-2019

*Dedicated to
Vonda's Posse*

Remembering Vonda
1948–2019

Edited by
Stephanie A. Smith
&
Jeanne Gomoll

UNIONSTREET**PRESS**

Remembering Vonda, edited by Stephanie A. Smith and Jeanne Gomoll,
© 2019 by Stephanie A. Smith and Jeanne Gomoll

Cover art and book design by Jeanne Gomoll

"The Wild Winds of Possibility:
Vonda N. McIntyre's *Dreamsnake*," by Ursula K. Le Guin, p. 19.
Originally published in *Cascadia Subduction Zone*, April 2011.

"Vonda N. McIntyre (1948–2019)," by L. Timmel Duchamp, p. 32.
Originally posted on *Ambling Along the Aqueduct*, Tuesday, April 2, 2019.

"Comic Legends: How Vonda N. McIntyre's First Name for Sulu Became Canon,"
by Brian Cronin, p. 48.
Originally posted on *CBR.com*, April 14, 2019.
https://www.cbr.com/star-trek-sulu-vonda-mcintyre-peter-david-first-name/

Sea Creature images, by Vonda N. McIntyre, p. 67.
http://www.vondanmcintyre.com/Index-BeadCreatures.html

Eileen Gunn, "A Remembrance of Vonda N. McIntyre," p. 88.
Leslie Howle, "Vonda N. McIntyre, Writer, Artist, and 'Mother of Writers,'" p. 92.
Paul Preuss, "Goodbye to Vonda," p. 101.
Tom Whitmore, "Remembering Vonda," p.136.
All originally published in *Locus Magazine*, May 2019.

Debbie Notkin & Laurie Toby Edison's joint tribute to Vonda, p. 103.
Originally published in *Body Impolitic*, Debbie Notkin and Laurie Toby Edison's blog.

Pamela Sargent's essay on McIntyre's *The Moon and the Sun*, p. 111.
Originally published by the Easton Press, as an introduction for a leather-bound edition of
The Moon and the Sun, part of the *Masterpieces of Science Fiction* series.
http://www.isfdb.org/cgi-bin/pubseries.cgi?49

"Tribute," by Nisi Shawl, p. 122.
Originally published in *The Seattle Times*, April 9, 2019

Paul Novitski interview of Vonda McIntyre, p. 144.
Originally published in *Starship*, spring 1979.

T. Jackson King's interview of Vonda N. McIntyre, p. 173.
Originally published by *Science Fiction Chronicle*, 1993.

"Vonda N. McIntyre, 1948–2019: Final Novel Adds to Seattle Science-Fiction Star's Legacy,"
by Alan Boyle, p. 192. Originally posted on *Geek Wire*, April 2, 2019.
https://www.geekwire.com/2019/
vonda-n-mcintyre-1948-2019-seattle-science-fiction-star-dies-cancer/

"I Will Walk With You," by Vonda N. McIntyre, p. 196.
Originally posted on *Bookview Café*, April 15, 2015.
https://booviewcafe.com/blog/2015/04/15/I-will-walk-with-you

"The Story of Why Vonda Wrote Starfarers," by Vonda N. McIntyre, p. 199.
Originally posted on *My Book the Movie*, December 23, 2009.
http://mybookthemovie.blogspot.com/2009/12/vonda-mcintyres-starfarers.html

Cover image based on photo of Vonda on Crete, at Phasistos.
Photo by Alice Lengers. Art by Jeanne Gomoll.

Union Street Press
jg@unionstreetdesign.com

First Edition
ISBN 978-0-359-69797-7

Remembering

- 3 **Clarion & Clarion West**
  - 4 Lyman Caswell
  - 5 Marilyn Holt
  - 9 John Walters

- 13 **Friendship with Ursula K. Le Guin**
  - 14 Arwen Curry
  - 15 Molly Gloss
  - 19 Ursula K. Le Guin
  - 24 Stephanie A. Smith

- 29 **The 70's Wave of Feminist SF & Beyond...**
  - 30 Rhonda Boothe
  - 32 L. Timmel Duchamp
  - 37 Jeanne Gomoll
  - 40 Ian K. Hagemann
  - 41 Susan Rubinyi-Anderson

- 45 **Star Trek**
  - 46 Tanya Avakian
  - 48 Brian Cronin
  - 50 Eric R. Franklin
  - 51 Sarah Grant
  - 52 Ole Kvern

- 55 **Book View Café & Other Support for Writers**
  - 56 Amy Sterling Casil
  - 61 Gregory Frost
  - 62 Deborah Ross
  - 64 Nancy Jane Moore

- 67 **Beaded Sea-Creatures**
  - 68 Julie E. Coryell
  - 70 Ctein
  - 71 Donna Haraway
  - 72 Karen Dawn Plaskon
  - 73 Lynn Johanna a.k.a. Lady Willow

- 75 **Memories & Legacies**
  - 76 Alma Alexander
  - 80 Gary L. Benson
  - 82 Liz Carey
  - 82 Frank Catalano
  - 82 Eli Cohen
  - 83 Frances Collin
  - 85 Jack Dann
  - 86 Doctor Science
  - 86 Ellen Eades
  - 86 Anthony Evans
  - 86 Deb Geisler
  - 87 Glenn Glazer
  - 87 William Grabowski
  - 87 Susan Gray
  - 88 Eileen Gunn
  - 90 Fonda Lee
  - 91 JLH
  - 92 Leslie Howle
  - 95 Kevin Kuenkler
  - 95 John Lorentz
  - 97 Kate MacDonald
  - 100 Sharan Newman
  - 101 Paul Preuss
  - 103 Debbie Notkin & Laurie Toby Edison
  - 107 Cat Rambo
  - 107 Neil Rest
  - 108 Robert Reynolds
  - 108 Candace Robb

108	Robyn	143	*Interviews*	
109	Jennifer Roberson		144	Paul Novitski
109	Carol Ryles		173	T. Jackson King
109	Geoff Ryman			
111	Pamela Sargent	187	*Obituaries*	
119	Kate Schaefer		188	Tom Whitmore
122	Nisi Shawl		192	Alan Boyle
126	Sylvi Shayl			
127	Jon Singer	195	*And In Her Own Words*	
128	Jon Singer			
130	Pam Smith		196	Vonda N. McIntyre
131	Stephanie A. Smith		199	Vonda N. McIntyre
132	Stephanie A. Smith			
133	Sara Stamey	205	*Early Years, Family*	
133	Sheree Renée Thomas	213	*Bibliography*	
133	Tamara Vining			
133	Donna J. Wagner	219	*Contributors Index*	
134	Cynthia Ward			
136	Tom Whitmore	223	*About this Book*	
137	Graham Watt			
139	Eric Williams	226	*Back Cover*	
139	Chris Willrich			
140	Amy Wolf	226	*Back Cover*	
142	Sara Yake		226	Jenny Islander

Clarion &
Clarion West

VONDA MCINTYRE was the first science fiction author I ever met. I spoke with her about my writing ambitions and she directed me to Clarion West. My participation in Clarion West was one of the finest experiences of my life. Thank you, Vonda. 𝒱

Lyman Caswell

Cartoon by Don Simmons. Originally published in *Janus 11*, which was also the program book for WisCon 2 (1978), at which Susan Wood and Vonda N. McIntyre were guests of honor.

Marilyn Holt
Memories of Vonda

I KNEW VONDA FOR WELL OVER FORTY YEARS. When we met is lost in the haze of time. I met her about the time that her first novel, *The Exile Waiting* (1975) was going to come out. About the same time, she stayed in Ursula K. Le Guin's cabin and wrote *Dreamsnake* (1978).

In 1979, Vonda returned from Brighton (UK) in the 37th Worldcon, Seacon '79. Someone had given her a set of cassette tapes of *The Hitchhiker's Guide to the Galaxy* from the BBC to give to her agent to give to Christopher Reeve's agent under the misbegotten idea that the U.S. was small and everyone knew one another. Vonda and I had gone out to dinner and she was telling me about her adventures. She wanted to hear the tapes (this was the first I had heard of the show or books), but neither of us had a cassette player, except that I had one in my car. So we listened to them all, all, sitting in front of her house in the middle of the night. It was autumn. The temperature dropped, the windows fogged over, and somehow we didn't run down the car battery. A police car cruised us several times, but we were sitting in a newish Saab, each in her own seat, not smoking, and laughing a lot. Soon after, the tapes went off to her agent, and we hoped that Christopher Reeve enjoyed them as much as we did.

At the end of 1982, J.T. Stewart and I decided to revive Clarion West. We had been doing a science fiction fair for Seattle Central Community College (SCCC), and this led to us being at Vonda's one day with David Hartwell, who was wearing a dashing charcoal gray with red and blue threads suit, and a New York City businessman's tie. David pitched that there was significant demand for another science fiction and fantasy workshop and that Clarion West should be revived. He made the point that new writers needed to be more dynamic and more adventuresome. He pointed out that Vonda took her fiction into uncharted territory in terms of social interaction.

While we were kicking ideas around at her dining table, as I remember, she was writing in her office, which shared a wall with the dining room. It was a hot, sunny day. She joined us for a brief break, and for the first time of many times told us that this would consume our lives. We did it, anyway.

Working with SCCC for class space, Western Washington University for upper division college credit, and Seattle University for housing, we went crazy. Vonda was a night owl, so when J.T. and I were in need of mental sustenance or relief, we would visit Vonda. She plied us with wine or coffee, or both, depending on what we needed. In wry humor, she would tell us that she knew a very good psychiatrist who could help us abandon Clarion West, and then we would get back to planning or just bitching about the whole process.

Vonda helped us identify the first instructors, and pulled Harlan Ellison in, to get Arthur Byron Cover and Norman Spinrad. She also told us what had been very hard for her to cope with at the University of Washington and the first three years of Clarion West, 1971, 1972, and 1973. Her support, help, faith, and friendship with the attendees made Clarion West a powerhouse.

Vonda owned the first personal computer that I actually met and used. She traveled and wrote so she bought the first portable computer, an Osborne. It had eight-inch floppy disks and a screen the size of a small smartphone. She left me to play with it while she went off and made dinner, after removing the floppy disk that held her work. I was in love even though I didn't have the manual. She kept after me to buy a personal computer because she knew first hand that I could not type a clean manuscript. Within a few months, I followed her advice.

In 2005, Vonda and I were talking about my farm. She volunteered and made a lovely and effective website, working directly with the HTML as was her preference to the end. She would never accept any payment, so I took her meat and vegetables from our farm. We used it for years until major change forced us to redo it. By then, she was making websites for authors and working on Book View Café. 𝒱

Jeremy Robkin, Carol Severance, Vonda and Amy Thomson at a Clarion West party, 1984. Photo by Jill Zeller.

8 *Remembering Vonda*

Clarion SF Writers Workshop in 1970 (its last year in its original location, Clarion PA State College), Harlan Ellison and Samuel Delany were two of the instructors. With the aid of Clarion founder Robin Scott Wilson, Vonda started Clarion West and ran it for three years; when Marilyn Holt and J.T. Stewart decided to restart it in the 1980s, Vonda continued to advise and support the workshop. West. Photo by Jay Kay Klein.

1	Allen Reuben	7	Gerry Conway	13	Joe Manfredini
2	David J. Skal	8	Lynn Marron	14	Mel Gilden
3	Dan Claxton	9	Debbie Goldstein	15	Jack Stahlman
4	Vonda N. McIntyre	10	Jean Mark Gawron	16	Steve Herbst
5	Ralph Benko	11	Russell Bates	17	Octavia Estelle Butler
6	Lucy Seaman	12	Jean Sullivan	18	Harlan Ellison

John Walters
Vonda and I

VONDA N. MCINTYRE played an integral part in my growth as a writer back in the early 1970s. If it were not for her resolve to initiate Clarion West in Seattle, I never would have attended Clarion—and I needed it badly. Not only did I need the critiquing, but I needed to know that there were other people who thought that writing was the best and most noble occupation in the universe.

I had foundered during my one year at Santa Clara University in California. I had missed classes; I had taken far too many drugs. The only positive thing that I took away from the experience was my resolve to be a writer. That happened quite unexpectedly. I enrolled in a class on science fiction as literature, and in the anthology textbook was a story called "I Have No Mouth and I Must Scream" by Harlan Ellison. By the time I finished reading that story I knew that I had to be a writer.

Fast forward to Seattle in the summer of 1972. I wanted to be a writer but I had no idea how to go about it. I was in a state of lassitude, still taking too many drugs and drinking too much as well. One day in the newspaper I came across an announcement that Harlan Ellison was doing a reading at the University of Washington. When I attended the reading, I learned about Clarion West, which until that time I had never heard of, and I became determined to attend the following year.

I applied and somehow was accepted into the Clarion West class of 1973. My teachers were Harlan Ellison, Ursula K. Le Guin, Joanna Russ, Terry Carr, Peter Beagle, and James Sallis. All thanks to Vonda's foresight and hard work in bringing Clarion West to Seattle.

After the 1973 workshop concluded, for a while I attended a critiquing group that met on Bubbles (Mildred Downey) Broxon's houseboat on Lake Union in Seattle. Vonda was there, and Bubbles, and F.M. Busby, and others.

Now there's a long break in my relationship with Vonda. In the mid-1970s, determined to find my unique voice as a writer, I took off on the road in search of inspiration and adventure. I traveled around Europe and journeyed across the Mideast to the Indian subcontinent. In short, I lived overseas for thirty-five years, in the process raising five sons. I also began to publish books and sell stories to magazines and anthologies.

In 2012, I returned to the states with some of my sons, recently divorced, a single parent, and struggling financially. Eventually I made my way back to Seattle.

Among the first science fiction conventions I ever attended was the Potlatch Convention in the University district. One evening I was socializing in the hospitality suite when who should I see across the room but Vonda. I went over and introduced myself. To be honest, I don't think she remembered me. After all, it had been about forty years since we'd last met. However, we had a great conversation. I asked about what had happened to past Clarion West acquaintances and filled her in on what I'd been up to over the years. I mentioned that I had recently read *The Moon and the Sun,* and she told me about the long and convoluted process of bringing that novel to the screen.

Over the summers following, I met Vonda several more times at gatherings of Clarion West alumni. We would share news and chat about what we were up to professionally.

The last time I saw Vonda was at one such gathering a couple of years ago. We were standing out on a terrace on a warm summer evening, and she said something that I have never forgotten. It lifted my spirits then and lifts them again whenever I think about it.

By that time I had published twenty-two or twenty-three books and almost seventy short stories. I told Vonda, "I still get far more rejections than acceptances."

She said, "I still get rejections too."

I was incredulous. Honestly, I could hardly believe it. This brilliant, multiple-award-winning writer still received rejections?

All I could say was, "really?"

"Oh yes," she said. "I get rejections all the time."

What Vonda's honesty did for my self-esteem was immeasurable. She didn't have to share that with me. I'm sure that there's no comparison between the amount of rejections I receive and the occasional one that she might have gotten, but that's not the point. I had thought that I was unique. I had thought that there was something wrong with me. She was telling me: hey, don't worry about it; it's just part of the job. It happens to all writers. Just hang in there and keep at it.

Vonda was always cheerful and uplifting. I'll miss our conversations.

Friendship with Ursula K. Le Guin

ON CAMERA IN *Worlds of Ursula K. Le Guin,* Vonda keenly describes the moment when women began to make a space for themselves in science fiction and fantasy, and the controversy it stirred up. I recorded her during a vacation with Ursula and Charles Le Guin in the southeast Oregon desert on a blistering day—a day so hot that the camera overheated and we had to pause filming and cool off. I still feel a little guilty about the heat of that afternoon, and grateful that she endured it.

Arwen Curry
director of the documentary film, *Worlds of Ursula K. Le Guin*

Vonda and Ursula. Ursula K. Le Guin won the Grand Master Award from SFWA, April 17, 2003, but was unable to attend, so Eileen Gunn accepted on her behalf. Ursula received her prize and was crowned at Potlatch in Seattle 2004. Photo by Kate Schaefer.

Molly Gloss
Vonda N. McIntyre—A Few Random Memories

IT WAS URSULA WHO INTRODUCED ME TO VONDA, though I can't remember the actual circumstances. Maybe it was at Westercon? or Orycon? Or maybe Vonda had come down from Seattle on the train and Ursula had asked me to drive the two of them somewhere? In any case, it was Ursula's style to introduce her younger writer friends to others of her younger writer friends—widening the circle, helping us find our tribe, our community, especially if we were feeling somewhat alone in this weird writing life.

In the years that followed, whenever I came up to Seattle for anything—a con, a bookstore event, a workshop—I stayed with Vonda in her spare bedroom. First time I visited, it seemed to me that she must have only just moved in—boxes not yet unpacked, pictures not yet hung, furniture haphazardly arranged as if the movers had just set it down anywhere. But of course that was Vonda, and even twenty years later the only picture she had hung on the wall was her prized original oil painting, the cover art for her novel *The Moon and the Sun*.

In recent years, she renovated the basement of her home into a rather upscale guest suite, and I know she hosted a lot of visiting writers there, including Clarion West faculty. I stayed in that suite a couple of times, and I remember the bathroom had a lovely shower. But I still missed the shower curtain in the upstairs bath, decorated with a not-to-scale solar system.

About eighteen years ago Ursula and Charles began asking me along when they were on their summer-rambles—I could be a relief driver for Charles, they said—and left unsaid that my husband had died recently and I no longer had a relief driver of my own for road trips. And soon our threesome became a foursome, as Vonda and I had become friends and were perfectly comfortable sharing a motel room. Those were some of the most memorable trips of my life. We all flew to Phoenix, rented a car and spent two weeks wandering around every corner of the Four Corners. We drove the North Cascades highway, a long loop east to the cowboy town of Winthrop, and down into the orchard country of central Washington. We made the long drive from Portland to San Jose when Ursula's work was the focus at some convention or other. I know there were other trips as well, and I wish I could ask Vonda or Ursula for a nudge to my memory.

Everyone knows Vonda was a night owl—it was typical for her to be at her computer into the wee dawn hours, and not rouse from bed until noonish or later. But when we were on a road trip, she adjusted her schedule with seemingly little trouble. In the bedroom she and I shared, we'd lie on our beds talking a long while, as if we were at a teen slumber party, but turn off the light by eleven o'clock. And she'd be up for breakfast by eight with the rest of us. I never asked her about it, but given the ease with which she changed her sleeping patterns I always imagined she must be someone who would never suffer jet lag.

Left to right: Octavia Butler, Kelly Link, Gavin Grant, Vonda N. McIntyre, Nina Kiriki Hoffman, L. Timmel Duchamp, Ted Chiang, Pat Murphy, Eileen Gunn, Leslie What, Molly Gloss, and (seated) Geoff Ryman, at a Clarion West gathering in Seattle, 2004. Photo by Neile Graham.

On those road trips, Vonda did most of the driving, only occasionally spelled by me or by Charles. She preferred to be in control of the wheel, and since she was an excellent driver none of us objected. She absolutely hated tail-gaters, but road rage wasn't her style. She always looked for the first safe place to pull over so she could grumblingly let them speed ahead of her.

She loved tech gadgets, and was an early adopter of GPS. On our trip to Phoenix, she programmed her new portable GPS (she named the thing Miss Thing) to take us to each day's destination. Ursula didn't trust the new-fangled thing—she much preferred reading a paper map—and indeed Miss Thing more than once took us wrong. But Vonda was determined to give it a fair and complete test run. "Don't be mad at Miss Thaaang," she'd say, completely unruffled, whenever we were sent the wrong way. "She's still in beta, her little brain will eventually figure it out."

I miss her. Vonda, that is, not Miss Thing. My GPS still sends me wrong sometimes, but Vonda never did. ⱽ

Vonda at Bandelier National Monument, near Los Alamos. Vonda, Charles and Ursula traveled through New Mexico and had a great time. Kate Schaefer writes: "The main thing I remember her reporting from the trip was that Vonda insisted that they rent a larger car than they had rented on previous trips, with plenty of room for passengers and luggage. 'We can afford to be comfortable,' she said. They all had long-standing habits of thrift." Photographer unknown.

Ursula K. Le Guin
The Wild Winds of Possibility:
Vonda N. McIntyre's Dreamsnake

Originally published in *Cascadia Subduction Zone*, April 2011.

DREAMSNAKE IS IN SOME WAYS A STRANGE BOOK, unlike any other in science fiction, which may explain the even stranger fact that it's not currently in print (except on line at https://bookviewcafe.com/bookstore/book/Dreamsnake/).

When people ask me what SF books influenced me or what are my favorites, I always mention *Dreamsnake*. Invariably I get a warm response—"oh yes!" and people still tell me how much the book meant to them when they first read it and ever since. But these days, many younger readers don't know it exists.

The short story the book was based on won the 1973 Nebula; the book was an immediate success; it became and still is beloved. Its moral urgency and rousing adventure story are not at all dated. It should have gone from one paperback reprint to another.

Why didn't it?

I have some theories.

THEORY #1: Ophidiophobia. The phobia is common and extends to pictures, even the mention, of snakes; and the book features them even in the title. A heroine who lets snakes crawl on her, and she's named Snake? Oh icky.

THEORY #2: Sex. It's an adult book. Snake, though, is barely more than a kid, setting out on her first trial of prowess, so that young women can and do identify with her, happily or longingly (and her taste in men is far better than that cavewoman Ayla's). But could the book be approved for use in schools? The sexual mores are as various as the societies, including some very unorthodox customs, and Snake's sexual behavior is both highly ethical and quite uninhibited. She can afford to be fearless, because her people know how to control their fertility through biofeedback, how to prevent insemination through a simple, learned technique. But, alas, we don't.... Given the relentless fundamentalist vendettas against "witchcraft" and "pornography" (read imaginative literature and sexual realism) in the schools, few teachers in the 1980s could invite the firestorm that might be started by a rightwing parent who got a hint of how young Snake was carrying on. Sexless hard-SF or Heinleinian fantasies of girlish docility were much safer. I think this killed the book's chance of being read widely as a text in junior high or high school, and even now may prevent its being marketed to the YA audience.

THEORY #3: the hypothesis of gendered reprinting. It appears that as a general rule books written by men get reprinted more frequently and over more years than books written by women. If this is so, Heinlein has always been given a handicap over McIntyre and will always have one.

Looking on the bright side, however, good writing tends to outlive mediocre writing, real moral questioning to outlast rant and wishful thinking. *Dreamsnake* is written in a clear, quick-moving prose, with brief, lyrically intense landscape passages that take the reader straight into its half-familiar, half-strange desert world, and fine descriptions of the characters' emotional states and moods and changes. And its generosity to those characters is quite unusual, particularly in science fiction with its tendency to competitive elitism.

Take the birth-control-via-biofeedback idea—certainly one of the great technological- imaginative inventions, and appreciated as such by many of McIntyre's readers (although because it's not hard tech and is subversive of gender dominance, male critics have tended to ignore it). McIntyre doesn't make it a subject of celebration, excitement, or question; it's taken for granted, it's how things are. Meeting a young man whose education has been so cruelly mismanaged that he doesn't know how to control his fertility, Snake is appalled, but sympathetic. She knows how bitterly humiliated he is by what he can see only as a personal failure, like impotence, but worse, because for him to have a heterosexual relation might involve damage to the other person...

They do manage to solve his problem.

Yes, there is some wishful thinking in McIntyre's book, but it is so thoroughly, carefully worked out in terms of social and personal behavior that its demonstration of a permanent streak of kindness in human nature is convincing—and as far from sentimentality as it is from cynicism.

The writer Moe Bowstern gave me a slogan I cherish: "subversion through friendliness." It looks silly till you think about it. It bears considerable thinking about. Subversion through terror, shock, pain is easy—instant gratification, as it were. Subversion through friendliness is paradoxical, slow acting, and durable.

And sneaky. A moral revolutionary, rewriting rules the rest of us were still following, McIntyre did it so skillfully and with such lack of self-promoting hoo-ha that we scarcely noticed. And thus she has seldom if ever received the feminist honors she is due, the credit owed her by writers to whom she showed the way.

What I mean by sneaky: take the character called Merideth. When I first read *Dreamsnake* I thought the odd spelling of the name Meredith was significant and tried so hard to figure out why this enigmatic, powerful person was called "merry death" that I totally missed what's really odd about Merideth. Three-cornered marriages being usual in this society, Merideth is married to a man and a woman...sure, fine...but we don't know whether as husband or as wife. We don't know Merideth's gender. We never do.

And I never noticed it till, in conversation about the book, I realized that I'd seen Merideth as a man—only because Meredith is a Welsh male name. There is no other evidence one way or the other, and McIntyre avoids the gender pronoun unerringly, with easy grace.

June Arnold's *The Cook and the Carpenter* came out in 1973 to much acclaim by feminists and was read mostly by feminists. *Dreamsnake* was published five years later as science fiction and read by everybody who read science fiction. How many of them even noticed that the gender of a character had been left up to them to decide, or refuse to decide? I still remember the shock of realizing that I'd been well and truly subverted. All the stuff we were saying about gender as social construct, as expectation, was revealed to me as built solidly into my own mind. And by that revelation my mind was opened.

I wish this beautiful, powerful, and highly entertaining book were back in print for the generation of SF readers who missed it, and all the young readers ready to have their mind blown wide open by the wild winds of possibility. *Dreamsnake* is a classic, and should be cherished as such.

Ursula K. Le Guin met Vonda N. McIntyre at an early SFWA meeting in Berkeley (Ursula's home town) when Ursula was thirtyish and the author of some but not yet innumerable books, and Vonda was, well she seemed about fifteen but must have been over twenty-one, because they went off together to the bar in the beautiful old Claremont Hotel, where they bonded. They have remained friends ever since, both in their daylight personas and as the shadowy, inscrutable figures of Ygor and Buntho, who do workshops, make books, hang curtains crooked, and send many, many emails between Portland and Seattle. Vonda is Ursula's extraordinary webmistress and Ursula lured Vonda into the National Writers Union. This disclosure is made in the interests of balanced review judgments: if Ursula did not admire Vonda's writing wholeheartedly, she wouldn't write about it.

Vonda, Carol Emshwiller, Eileen Gunn, Pat Murphy, and Ursula K. Le Guin, 2006, at WisCon 30. Photo by Jeanne Gomoll.

Stephanie A. Smith
And Here Be She-Dragons

DURING URSULA K. LE GUIN'S public memorial in Portland, as the red, glittering Chinese dragon made its serpentine, ceremonial way down the auditorium aisle, cymbals clashing, drums drumming, Vonda said she'd been thinking "wow, wouldn't it be neat if it coiled in on itself in a spiral, and then uncoiled?" "And then," she said at the after-party with complete, open and joyous delight, "it did! it did!" this, to me, is pure Vonda.

Ursula's memorial event was also the very last time I saw my teacher and friend of thirty some odd years. Yet, somehow, it seems fitting to me that the very first time we met, it was because of Ursula, and then that the very last time I would see my friend, it was also because of Ursula. When I was sixteen, and browsing in a bookstore during a lunch break from my job at Condé Nast in New York City, a stranger, a man with a white beard and a beret, who Vonda insisted must have been Damon Knight, reached over my shoulder and handed me *A Wizard of Earthsea*, saying he thought I'd like it.

And thus is a life altered.

Because of Ursula's book, I found my way to *Dreamsnake* and to *The Dancers of Arun*, and then, to my terrified delight, I was accepted by the 1981 summer PSU Haystack Writing Program, where Ursula K. Le Guin, Vonda N. McIntyre and Elizabeth Lynn would teach. In one summer, my far-off teenage idols became actual mentors. For the first few days, I was nearly catatonic with fear, hope, and joy, but Vonda's matter-of-fact, down-to-earth practical warmth anchored and steadied a terrified kid. She was ten years older than I, with bluer than blue eyes, talented, funny, awe-inspiring, whip-smart. What I learned in those three weeks can't be narrated; what I came to practice in the subsequent five years that I lived in Portland, I still practice today, every day.

At Ursula's suggestion, after Haystack, I moved from Boston to the Pacific Northwest, a newly minted, penniless B.A. in English and Latin with a portable typewriter and not much else. I was introduced to Vonda's alter ego Ygor, and to Ursula's, Buntho, and over the years, through Ygor and Buntho, to a number of other feminist SF/F writers. In my early twenties, I got to spend my days and some nights with what I'd dubbed to myself "the best company in the entire world," as I tried to navigate unknown territory, to grow my own wings and perhaps fly. For a few months, I dithered between living in Seattle or Portland, but Ursula found a job for me, so Portland became home. I shared a rental with other young women a few streets away from the Le Guins. In Ursula and Charles' home, both as an invited guest and as a house sitter, I drafted most of my first book, with Leonard the cat on my lap, and Mt. St. Helens in the distance. Ursula was the same age as my mother, and in her I found another; we shared Earl Gray tea and home-made *pfeffernusse*, learned t'ai chi together in the living room, listened to music, watched television.

But while I was still dithering about where to live, I stayed with Vonda. I remember distinctly that first morning. I got up as quietly as possible to use the bathroom; the shower curtain had the solar system on it; the towels were being warmed up by a towel-heater and I thought, "you are really in Vonda's house." I actually pinched myself.

We would talk, or not; Vonda made the best guacamole ever; we went out and played endless games of Pac-man or stayed at home with Jane Hawkins and Ole Kvern, to fool around on one of the first personal computers, Vonda's Osborne. Sometimes I answered the phone in the morning so that Vonda, sleeping, wouldn't be disturbed by the ring. Once, Harlan Ellison was on the line.

What I remember most, however, is all the laughter.

Ygor and Buntho knew how to laugh, how to make each other laugh, as Vonda said, "like loons." They knew how to enjoy life, more than anyone I've ever met or will ever meet. And although they could indulge relentlessly in serious silliness, neither Ygor nor Buntho would suffer fools gladly. When I sold my first novel, Ursula chuckled and said, with a mercurial little sparkle in her eye, "let's phone Vonda!" and so we did. Ygor and Buntho were so warm, so generous, and so marvelously talented; they fed both body and soul. When I was freezing my butt off during that first Portland winter, Vonda sent me first an electric blanket, and then one she'd crocheted; a twinkling sea-creature followed, along with phone calls or letters on life, love and always, on writing. For years, while I labored to earn a Ph.D. in California, then struggled to stay alive in academia in Florida, Vonda graciously read many pieces of fiction I wrote, including the novel I'm revising now, which she knew I would dedicate to her; she said simply of this last thing, "I enjoyed it."

Precious words.

But back when I was still more or less a child and struggling to draw up a life-map into adulthood, my friend Harriet said once that I should never be afraid, because these two women were looking out for me. There be she-dragons on that there old, worn map, I think, forever wise and wonderful.... *V*

A Winter Solstice Ritual from the Pacific Northwest

by

Ursula K. Le Guin
&
Vonda N. McIntyre

Vonda N McIntyre   *Ursula K. LeGuin*

YGOR AND BUNTHO
MAKE BOOKS
PRESS

Portland • Seattle

Ygor and Buntho (usually spelled with the N turned backwards) were the alter egos of Vonda and Ursula. They collaborated on chapbooks—Ygor and Buntho Make Books Press—Christmas cards and a host of silly antics, lined fully with the affection of a long and serious friendship.

Vonda, Carol Emshwiller, and Ursula K. Le Guin, 2006, at WisCon 30. Photo by Jeanne Gomoll.

The 70's Wave of Feminist SF & Beyond...

VONDA, I WAS so sad to hear how ill you are and how short your prognosis. I wish you joy and peace. You have made a big difference in my life! First when I read *Dreamsnake* in my early twenties in Boise, which I found in the tiny women's library my lesbian feminist friends started in our living room. Then, remarkably, you let me sleep in your spare bedroom when I moved to Seattle in 1984, if only because my best friend from high school was living with Jane in your basement at the time, but still, I was humbled. You even washed the sheets! I can't remember how long I stayed, but it was long enough to develop a secret crush on you as would befit a tenderhearted small-town twenty-something. I confess that I have foolishly felt a small degree of ownership for your increasing success ever since. Let me know if you need your sheets washed a few times—I owe you so much more than that! Much love.

Rhonda Boothe

Vonda holding the Locus Award, which she received in 1979 for *Dreamsnake*. The prize was a small wooden puzzle in the shape of a rocketship, 1979 Westercon. Photo by Andrew Porter.

L. Timmel Duchamp
Vonda N. McIntyre (1948-2019)

Originally posted on Ambling Along the Aqueduct, Tuesday, April 2, 2019

VONDA N. MCINTYRE DIED YESTERDAY. She was a person of many, albeit overlapping, communities, which makes it unusually difficult for me to give a sense of who she was in our world. The most visible aspect of her life, of course, is her published work, which includes *Dreamsnake* (winner of both the Hugo and Nebula awards for best novel), the fabulous historical science fiction novel *The Moon and the Sun* (winner of the Nebula award), a few other stand-alone novels, her four-novel *Starfarers* series, several *Star Trek* and *Star Wars* novels, and a host of short fiction, some of which was collected in *Fireflood and Other Stories*, and includes, from 2005, "Little Faces," which I especially loved, and which was a finalist for the Nebula and Sturgeon Awards.

Vonda was one of those authors whose work I read and loved long before I met her. In fact, her *Dreamsnake* was among the first science fiction books I ever read. I found it in a bookstore in Salt Lake City, when I was living there in 1978, and it gave me my very first taste of what I later came to call feminist SF. The idea of women being able to learn to control their reproduction through bio-control enchanted me (and instantly raised the bar for what I expected from science fiction texts), and made

Vonda, Karen Joy Fowler, and Kelly-Sue DeConnick, 2016, Tiptree Symposium, Portland OR. Photo by Jeanne Gomoll.

me hungry for more such imaginative approaches to biology—by which I mean the biology that society had told me was destiny—for girls and women. I suspect that that novel in particular helped prepare me for a different conceptualization of biology that I eventually picked up from feminist science studies. In short, I was an early fan of Vonda's. Much later, reading Joanna Russ' letters to Alice Sheldon (which can be found in the University of Oregon's special collections), I inferred, without surprise, that Joanna and Vonda must have had many intense conversations in the 1970s about all things feminist and science fictional because Joanna often referred to what Vonda had said about this or that when writing to Alli Sheldon.

I first saw Vonda in the flesh a few years later, after I'd moved to Seattle, at a women writers' conference (graced by such stars

Hand-painted art by Mary Prince, sold at WisCon 7, at the Tiptree Auction, 1983. Image provided by Darrah Chavey with permission from Mary Prince.

as Maya Angelou, Joanna Russ, Toni Cade Bambara, and Carolyn Forché). Vonda gave a reading as well as participated on a panel I attended. I don't think I'd ever before seen a woman wearing blue jeans and a blazer (which I'd often known male mathematicians and musicians to do), and seeing her do so instantly made me want to, also. What I recall most from both the panel and her reading was my impression of how deeply embedded her science fictional imagination was in her background in biology. She was, to me, a star in a dazzling firmament of stars—all women writers.

Later, of course, after Nicola Griffith dragged my isolated, introverted self into Seattle's community of SF writers, I came to know her, at first as a crusty, trenchantly witty personality and then as a generous force helping make things happen and run smoothly (always unobtrusively). She was, for instance, one of the founders of Clarion West. Later, she helped found the Book View Café and helped produce their e-books, which I became aware of only when Kath and I were referred to her for much-needed advice for Aqueduct. Her community was larger than these, though, as evidenced by her being a Guest of Honor at the 2015 Worldcon, held in Spokane.

I thought a great deal about her last month, while in Port Townsend, because I knew she had only weeks to live. I was stunned by the volume of memories I have of my encounters with her. Like many other people, I know, I'm thankful to have enjoyed her friendship and will miss her actively intelligent presence in the world. 𝒱

36   *Remembering Vonda*

Seated together on the grand stairway in the Madison Concourse Hotel lobby are the 32 of WisCon's returning guests of honor who attended WisCon 30 in May 2006. Vonda is seated in the second row, far left. Photo by Mary Langenfeld.

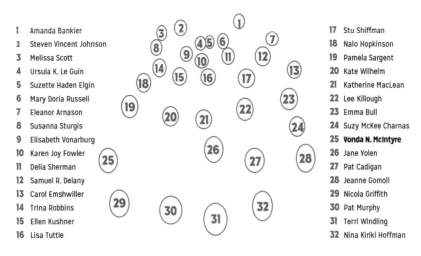

1 Amanda Bankier
2 Steven Vincent Johnson
3 Melissa Scott
4 Ursula K. Le Guin
5 Suzette Haden Elgin
6 Mary Doria Russell
7 Eleanor Arnason
8 Susanna Sturgis
9 Elisabeth Vonarburg
10 Karen Joy Fowler
11 Delia Sherman
12 Samuel R. Delany
13 Carol Emshwiller
14 Trina Robbins
15 Ellen Kushner
16 Lisa Tuttle

17 Stu Shiffman
18 Nalo Hopkinson
19 Pamela Sargent
20 Kate Wilhelm
21 Katherine MacLean
22 Lee Killough
23 Emma Bull
24 Suzy McKee Charnas
25 **Vonda N. McIntyre**
26 Jane Yolen
27 Pat Cadigan
28 Jeanne Gomoll
29 Nicola Griffith
30 Pat Murphy
31 Terri Windling
32 Nina Kiriki Hoffman

Jeanne Gomoll

IN 1969, MY COLLEGE FRESHMAN LIT PROFESSOR suggested that I write a paper on one of my favorite writers, Robert Heinlein, and focus on his philosophy and politics. It turned out that Ms. Dean was employing a subtle strategy to shatter my affection for Heinlein. Well, her diabolical plan worked perfectly. By the time I was through examining Heinlein's fiction in the way she'd proposed, I was angry at myself and totally through with Heinlein. After that, I read very little SF during my college years. But in 1975, a couple years after I graduated, I noticed some interesting names appearing on book covers in the local bookstore—women's names. Hmmm.... I offered some suggestions to my feminist reading group.

Soon after, I joined a local SF group that called itself Madstf and we published a fanzine called *Janus*. One of the first book reviews I wrote for *Janus* compared Vonda N. McIntyre's *The Exile Waiting* and Le Guin's *The Dispossessed*. These books thrilled me. The authors were obviously feminists, actually using science fiction to imagine egalitarian futures. It's hard to remember just how really new that felt to me, how different the world was then, that simply choosing a strong, woman protagonist felt fresh and unexpected. Of course, I learned subsequently, about all the women writers who had come before, but at the time, to me, it felt like a whole new world opening. I was struck by how both McIntyre and Le Guin's protagonists abandoned worlds in which they felt trapped in order to develop their strength, but then finally returned home again, strong enough to re-make their worlds. I began to articulate a theory that SF was the ideal tool for feminist change.

I continued to work on our fanzine, reviewing McIntyre and Le Guin and Russ and Charnas and and and. *Janus* eventually became *Aurora*. And we decided to put on a feminist-oriented SF convention—WisCon, which is still alive and kicking forty-three years later. In 1978 we invited Vonda N. McIntyre to WisCon 2 as our guest of honor (with Susan Wood). And then we invited Vonda back to WisCon 10, WisCon 20 and WisCon 30.

Drawing upon her college work in biology and genetics, Vonda ignored the transparently sexist preference for so-called "hard SF" vs. the so-called "soft SF," such as fiction based on biological and genetic sciences. She was one of the first women SF writers of the 1970 whose fiction explored gender roles, sexuality, and human relationships from a feminist perspective.

Thrilling as it was to read Vonda and the other revolutionary women writers of the time, I was entirely gobsmacked to actually meet her and get to know her as a friend. Vonda's characters helped me see a wider horizon of futures for our world; Vonda herself, as a person, helped me recognize an unlimited range of possible futures for myself, because of how she took charge of her life and helped change the field of science fiction.

In fact, with Vonda's recommendation, her sister Carolyn offered me a job producing a marine supply catalog. If it weren't for the fact that I received my dream-job offer that very same week (graphic designer, Wisconsin Department of Natural Resources), I would probably have moved to Seattle in the summer of 1979. I will always be grateful for that, but even more so for knowing Vonda as a friend for all these decades. 𝒱

Vonda reading at WisCon 2. Photo by Diane Martin.

Ian K. Hagemann

BACK IN THE LATE 1990S, I was at an informal gathering of local science fiction folks that Vonda regularly hosted. One evening, a rather loud-mouthed white male attendee started to complain that he was no longer free to express himself due to the alleged need to be "politically correct." This wasn't a sentiment that was usually expressed at those parties (or in Vonda's home), but Vonda's riposte was gracious and thoughtful. Rather than argue the merits of his assertions, Vonda reminded him that white men such as himself had always been free to express themselves: the difference was that others who had been previously silenced were now free to express themselves as well. He might not like what he was hearing in response, but he was now able to receive new kinds of feedback about the impact of his words that he was free to incorporate if he chose to do so. But if he chose not to behave differently, then it was reasonable to believe that he was being intentionally rude and disrespectful.

What I like about this response (which I've used quite a bit in the intervening years) is how disarming it is. By underlining his agency in how to react, it sidesteps the various "fragilities" that can get instilled in people with unearned privilege while still educating them about how to behave better and therefore holding them accountable for the impact of their words. I only wish that I were that articulate more of the time myself. 𝒱

Susan Rubinyi-Anderson
The Making of Aurora: Beyond Equality

AT FIRST GLANCE, Vonda and I might have seemed like an unusual duo to co-edit one of the first women in science fiction anthologies, *Aurora: Beyond Equality*. Vastly dissimilar in multiple respects (background, personality, perspective) we could have easily come from separate planets or perhaps even parallel universes. I had just finished my Master's in comparative literature, French, and Russian. Soon to be an ex-graduate student in genetics, at our first meeting, Vonda was complaining in a frustrated tone: "My cells won't clone."

A few months later, as I was developing the first women in SF course at the University of Washington, a new idea occurred to me: "what about us co-editing a feminist SF anthology of original stories to encourage writers to envisage wider possibilities for both women and men?"

I saw the combination of Vonda's and my different backgrounds as a potential strength for helping transform my vision into reality.

It wasn't easy to get her buy-in. She immediately came up with a whole list of reasons why it would never work.

"Neither of us has yet published a full-length book" was one of her arguments.

"So what?" I countered.

Since I'm by nature optimistic (probably a result of having read *Pollyanna* too many times as a child), I persisted. Finally she agreed.

"You have a background in literature, you write the proposal," she insisted.

"Ok, no problem."

Since she had a larger network of professional contacts in SF publishing, she took over the research into possible markets. Our combined efforts paid off when the proposal I'd written was accepted. Four years later, after both of us reading myriad submissions, *Aurora: Beyond Equality* appeared. Probably few readers noticed a curious anomaly. Inside the cover, my name came first, on the cover, Vonda's preceded mine, perhaps reflecting the fact she'd just sold her first novel to our publishers. So I got a small taste of why order of billing is so important to Hollywood writers!

Not only was our anthology well received, one of the stories by James Tiptree Jr. won both a Hugo and a Nebula. This leads me to our discovering afterwards that a literary hoax had been played on us. We had painstakingly tried to embody the idea of equality by choosing fifty percent of the stories written by women, fifty percent by men. In addition to Tiptree's award-winning story, we'd also selected one by a Racoona Sheldon, typed in an unusual blue ink, a new unknown writer. As we later found out, she and James Tiptree Jr. were one and the same person, both pseudonyms of Dr. Alice Sheldon.

I see the fact that both female protagonists and writers are now commonplace as a measure of the trailblazing success of our anthology, *Aurora: Beyond Equality*, named for the goddess of the dawn. 𝒱

Vonda in Versailles, for the filming of *The King's Daughter*, 2014.
Photo by Sean McNamara.

Star Trek

Tanya Avakian

VONDA N. MCINTYRE was the first science fiction writer I read. In 1983, I found her novelization of *Star Trek II: The Wrath of Khan*. I found the rest of Vonda's work in short order and fell in love. Her prose was exquisite; her characterization was subtle and completely original; the moral depth at which she rendered the story and compelled the reader to follow her was daunting, painful, gentle, and beguiling all at once. From Vonda I went on to Le Guin, Russ, Tiptree and the rest of the feminist science fiction canon at the time. All great writers; all great in their own way; but before I knew any of that I knew they came recommended by Vonda. I would not meet her until some twenty years in the future, at WisCon. We shared several WisCons, and she always greeted me with recognition and a smile. I tried to make beaded sea creatures in a workshop together with her; suffice it to say her fame in that area remained safe. I have one of her creatures at home, purchased in a charity auction. It is very precious.

For a few years before my first WisCon I corresponded with her through her sff.net community. Her friendly reserve made it easy to talk to her in any situation, less easy to know her judgments. She was a generous judge of character but not infinitely so, and it was at times awkward to chat through the background of sheer emotion created by her stories. At times one knew she had noticed something that bemused her about oneself; at times, something that displeased her. The death of Jesse in *Dreamsnake*, Snake's final triumph, Mischa's torture in sensory deprivation; they were there at such times. It was hard to tell if she knew or if it mattered. It was always possible to know when she was delighted, blessedly. She was full of amusement when I described the White House Christmas tree as "the Christmas comb jelly." She was intrigued at the suggestion of the young Lili Taylor to play Snake, and she was unreservedly sympathetic about all the little vicissitudes of life, going on at the same time.

Now that it can't embarrass her, I'll close by naming two songs that always made me think of Vonda from my teenage years on: Arlo Guthrie's "Darkest Hour," which sounds like a Vonda story in verse, and Judy Collins' "Houses," which simply expressed how I always felt about her:

> *You were always flying*
> *Nightingale of sorrow,*
> *Singing bird with rainbows on your wings.* 𝒱

Vonda at the University Bookstore in Seattle, February 7, 2018. Vonda was part of a group reading for B Cubed Press—"A Modest Proposal for the Perfection of Nature." Photo by K.G. Anderson.

Brian Cronin
Comic Legends: How Vonda N. McIntyre's First Name for Sulu Became Canon

Originally posted on CBR.com, April 14, 2019. Peter David's comic book adaptation of *Star Trek VI* helped to get Vonda N. McIntyre's first name for Sulu made canon.

THE WORLD OF SCIENCE FICTION lost a great voice when the amazing Vonda N. McIntyre passed away earlier this month. McIntyre was a multiple Nebula-award-winning author, with her novel, *Dreamsnake*, capturing both the 1979 Nebula award and the 1979 Hugo award.

She was also an acclaimed writer of *Star Trek* novels (she wrote the novelizations for three of the first four *Star Trek* films; Gene Roddenberry adapted the first one himself.).

She wrote one of the earliest original *Star Trek* novels, the beloved *The Entropy Effect*.

In that novel, she gave Sulu the first name of Hikaru....

There was a bit of a kerfuffle at the time about whether she was even allowed to do that, which she explained to IO9 a while back:

"The only potential glitch in the *Star Trek* books came about because I couldn't figure out how to write a love scene where the protagonists called each other by their surnames. So I gave Mr. Sulu a first name, "Hikaru," which is from *The Tale of Genji*. I was blissfully unaware of the glitch till long after the fact;

someone at Paramount objected to the idea of the character's having a given name, for reasons unclear to me. David had the good idea of asking Gene Roddenberry and George Takei their opinion, and both of them said 'go for it' or words to that effect. And so Mr. Sulu has a first name."

However, while the name was allowed for the novel, Sulu continued to be just called "Sulu" in the *Star Trek* films.

This changed with the help of Peter David.

David, of course, was an acclaimed writer of *Star Trek* novels and comics. His original *Star Trek* run for DC saw him do some Sulu character development…

Later, David was doing the comic book adaptation of *Star Trek VI* (after also adapting *Star Trek V*), which is where director Nicholas Meyer finally allowed Sulu to become a Captain…

Well, David was obviously familiar with McIntyre's work and after visiting the set of the film, he persuaded Meyer to add "Hikaru" to the film and Meyer did so. It, of course, was also in David's adaptation…so Sulu's first name was now canon! Very cool stuff. A nice tribute to a wonderful writer. Vonda N. McIntyre will be greatly missed. 𝒱

Star Trek novels by Vonda N. McIntyre—*The Entropy Effect*, 1981; *The Wrath of Khan*, 1982; *The Search for Spock*, 1984; *Enterprise: The First Adventure*, 1986.

LIKE SEVERAL OTHERS, here, *Star Trek* was my path into fandom. As a voracious reader, I read a metric fuckton of *Trek* novels in my pre-teen and early teen years (and, if I'm being painfully honest, through today, thirty years past my teen years). I was not a very discriminating reader, either. If it had *Star Trek* on the cover, I would read it. *Enterprise: The First Adventure* was heavily advertised as being somehow special among *Trek* novels—unlike most of the Pocket Books of the line (at the time), it wasn't numbered. And it was one of the better books in the series. Even as a non-discriminating consumer of books, I noticed how much better it was. Her novelizations of the films were (especially in the case of *III*) frequently better than the films themselves. She will be very much missed.

Eric R. Franklin

I'VE BEEN A FAN of Vonda's since I started reading *Star Trek* books in the late 1980s; I've read the *Starfarers* series, as well as all the *Star Trek* books she wrote. Now I'm on the hunt for everything else she ever wrote as well. My story is pretty simple, and not terribly interesting as these things go. I met Vonda at Wayward Coffeehouse in Seattle a few years ago at a reading of stories inspired by Octavia Butler's life and writings. I worked at the coffeehouse at the time, and it was the first event I was in charge of—so I was a little nervous. I knew Vonda was coming, which made me even more nervous, because I was getting to actually meet her! When she walked in I knew exactly who she was. I went over to greet her, and I think I was pretty cool and collected for the most part…and then I proceeded to quietly (hopefully!!) gush praise at her for at least a couple of minutes. Vonda thanked me for my words and shook my hand, and she was so sweet and gracious; I don't actually remember much of the rest of the evening, other than that I was on cloud nine.

Sarah Grant

Ole Kvern

WHAT I REMEMBER IS THAT VONDA WAS DITHERING about taking on the contract for *The Wrath of Khan* because the proposed deadline was very tight. There wasn't enough time to type more than one draft of a manuscript on her IBM Selectric, and she didn't want to take on a job where she could only write one draft. Jane (Hawkins) convinced her that there were affordable personal computers just coming onto the market, and that with "word processing software" (a phrase that was new to us at the time—this was 1981), she'd be able to complete more drafts in the time allowed. They pooled their funds to buy an Osborne-1.

The Osborne-1 wasn't much to look at—it looked like a portable sewing machine. It had a white (or was it green?) phosphor 3.5-inch CRT display and ran the CP/M operating system. The micro-controller chips in our toasters today have more computing power. But it did have WordStar. We all started learning WordStar.

Vonda's editors would not accept manuscripts that weren't typed on an IBM Selectric, so we bought a daisywheel printer, a Diablo 630. Jane and I tweaked WordStar's output settings so that it was close enough to IBM Selectric output that it was acceptable to the editor. I still don't know if we fooled them, or if they just decided to let it pass.

We fed Vonda while she was working on the novelization. Mostly chicken paprika (which she'd taught me how to cook) and her secret spinach salad (which she taught me how to make). Then we helped with entering some of the final copy editing changes and getting the manuscript out of the printer.

What it meant to Vonda was that she was able to get the manuscript in on time, in a form that was acceptable to her. The book then spent some time on the *New York Times* bestseller list. And it was a pretty good book! If she'd had control of the script, it would have been better, of course, but she took a run-of-the-mill Hollywood plot and turned it into something much more interesting.

That introduction to computing surprised me. I had always thought of myself as an intuitive (i.e., not analytical) person. Learning to work with software—even the crude computing tools that we had then—was a revelation. Working with software and hardware felt a lot like creating artwork. For me, the intuitive and the analytical were basically the same—that the feeling of creating artwork and the feeling of solving the riddle of an obscure "dot command" in WordStar were identical.

Would I have had what I jokingly refer to as "my career" (almost 40 years in computers/software, and counting) had it not been for Vonda, Jane, and *The Wrath of Khan*? I doubt it. 𝒱

Vonda speaking at a panel at the Tiptree Symposium: "Ursula K. Le Guin and the Field of Feminist Science Fiction". University of Oregon, Eugene, 2016. Photo by Nina Kiriki Hoffman.

Book View Café & Other Support for Writers

Amy Sterling Casil
What is Book View Café, How Did It Start, and Why Did Vonda Support It?

IF, AFTER YOU HEARD of Vonda N. McIntyre's illness or death, you decided to buy one of her e-books, you would find you could only buy one through Book View Café's e-book store, not on Amazon.com or other commercial e-book stores.

So, what is Book View Café (BVC)? Vonda, Ursula K. Le Guin, and about 12 other female science fiction and fantasy writers, led by Sarah Zettel, formed a cooperative association in 2006 or so. You likely don't know who I am, but I was one of them. I was Book View Café's incorporating Treasurer and am still the Treasurer.

BVC was one of the first author publishing cooperatives. It has grown to more than fifty members. Now, authors of any gender identification are members and our president is Steven Harper Piziks. Steven was the first male author to join BVC and we dubbed him "Igor," a moniker he continues to accept with good humor.

But when BVC started, it was inspired by discussions about the publishing industry that we had on our all-female-identifying SF/F author email discussion list: the SF-FFW's (science fiction-fantasy female writers). All of the founding members of that e-mail list and BVC were female SF/F writers. BVC's most famous founding member was Ursula K. Le Guin. Our best, most beloved founding member was and always will be, Vonda.

In those early days, I remember a conversation with Vonda about her experiences in Hollywood screenwriting. Another of our friends and another founding member, Sherwood Smith, also had many experiences writing for film and television. I had just completed writing some film tie-in books (none of which have my name on them).

I didn't realize until that conversation how close Vonda had come to becoming a famous, rich Hollywood script writer and how much poorer our world was because that hadn't happened. It was one of the first times I realized the severity and depth of unjustified gender bias in not just SF writing, but other types of writing and related creative endeavors.

For months, our email list that included some of the most famous, awarded female SF writers ever, had been rife with complaints about orphaned book series, editors being suddenly fired and leaving their posts and books behind, mysterious royalty statements of dubious provenance, and the general difficulty of being a female SF/F writer in any capacity. In addition to Ursula K. Le Guin and Vonda, other well-known and successful list members included Anne McCaffrey. Probably you have heard of her.

In our e-mail discussions, Vonda was always very equitable and very professional. Unlike some who may have angrily decried the unfairness of it all and bitterly lamented orphaned book series, horrendous book covers with bug-eyed monsters slapped on fantasy series or vice-versa, and lackluster (who am I kidding?—non-existent)—book promotion. I kept my troubles to myself more than most people likely knew, but I also had insights from being a nonprofit executive, SFWA treasurer, and an insider in several small- to medium-publishing companies. My fiancé Alan Rodgers had been an editor for *Twilight Zone* and *Night Cry* magazines and was a former *New York Times* bestselling author. He was a partner with John Betancourt in Wildside Press. I attended meetings and had even been to an Amazon "insiders" meeting where I had heard juicy details about what the—at the time, upstart—online bookseller was willing to offer writers: seventy percent royalties. The legacy publishers we were familiar with were offering ten percent royalties on e-books.

There were all generations of writers on the list. "We don't have to sit around and take what they're dishing out to us any more," I said one day. Soon the list was buzzing with ideas and writers with organizational skills like Sarah Zettel stepped forward to get the project off the ground.

BVC selected the cooperative association as its model. Pati Nagle, another gifted writer with organizational skills, became the incorporating president when it came time to make things official and legal.

BVC is an author cooperative which means that membership isn't about just publishing your books with the cooperative. Everyone in the association has a job—or more than one.

Vonda's job was formatting our books and uploading them to the bookstore. When we began, the process was a lot more challenging than it is today. There weren't programs that would just do it for you. Many members were non-technical and relied heavily on Vonda's expertise. She called the HTML, which is the basis of all e-books, "old high Martian."

Even though I could do it myself, I trusted Vonda more. Vonda typeset all of my BVC books.

One day, while working on my second collection, she dropped me a short note asking an editorial question. Being so accustomed to sloppy, hasty copy-editing and "reviews" by people who obviously never read past the first sentence or back cover copy, I found strange tears of surprise and gratitude streaking down my cheeks. Vonda was so thoughtful and caring. She would typeset our books but she also copyedited and watched for possible errors.

I remember corresponding with her about genetic defects. My baby Anthony had been born with Down syndrome. I can seriously barely write this right now.

If a question arose about taxes, corporate governance, or what the organization should or shouldn't do, Vonda would invariably respond, "that's above my pay grade."

But being a fully-realized human and a vastly gifted and brilliant writer was not above Vonda's pay grade. There was no pay grade for the type of woman, human, and writer Vonda was. Is.

She is one of the finest people I've ever known.

We started BVC because we—all of us—had no choice. We were not able to continue with our careers, none of us, without getting together and helping each other. BVC enabled so many members to put their backlist books back into print to a new readership. It was the precursor to indie publishing that many readers of this book may be familiar with today. You will find some of Vonda's books available in audio book form on Au-

Reading at University Book Store in Seattle, August 18, 2017. Photo by Amy Wolf.

dible because BVC did a catalog deal with them, but you will not find her e-books on Amazon because she, like Ursula K. Le Guin, did not support Amazon's lack of corporate responsibility and the harm the company has done to literature and ethical publishing.

Now, ten cents of every BVC book sale goes to the cooperative, and ninety cents goes to the author. The association allows its authors to support each other and earn money from sales of their books. That is why Vonda was one of the founders of BVC and gave so much of her time and life to it during the past eleven years. There is no day that goes by that I don't miss her or think of what a wonderful writer and person she was….she is with the stars now… *V*

Gregory Frost

I HAD KNOWN OF AND READ Vonda McIntyre for literal decades before I found myself joining Book View Café and formatting both my own and other author's books, and of course immediately running into problems. Vonda acted as the formatting gatekeeper, and we started having dialogues about which e-book-distilling programs added the most garbage code, and things like that. They were just wonderful chats and I'm glad I kept copies of some of them. She knew everything there was to know, and she shared it with such a sense of community and helpfulness that it almost made me want to have problems so as to have to query her. I guess the point is, she was such a steady, calm and wise voice, I simply took it for granted that she would be around forever. Her absence, even as this online presence, is quite palpable. *V*

Deborah Ross

MY FRIEND AND FELLOW WRITER, Vonda N. McIntyre, died last month. There were a bunch of obituaries, including mainstream papers like the *New York Times* and *The Guardian*, and many genre publications. Her friends have been gathering memories of her as well. It took me a while to pull together my thoughts, but here they are: I have been thinking what I could add to the wonderful stories about Vonda. She was one of the many amazing women writers who inspired my early career, but I didn't meet her in person until 1994, when she came to Los Angeles (where I lived then) for a fellowship to the Chesterfield Writer's Film Project workshop. How could I resist the chance to meet her? I wrote to her, introduced myself, and received a warm reply. I picked her up and brought her home to my family. I remember her relaxing, being treated as a normal but quite fascinating person, away from the artificial, competitive environment of Hollywood. We got together a number of times during her sojourn, talking a little about writing but mostly life and food and the weather, just enjoying each other's company. I remember her returning the favor when I was in Seattle for a convention and she took me out to the best salmon dinner I've had in my life. We found a lot to laugh about. Then when I joined Book View Café she was my mentor as well, endlessly patient and encouraging. (Plus I got to brag that she formatted my e-books, how amazing!)

One particular discussion stands out from her time in LA. The topic had gotten on to media tie-ins and shared worlds (she'd written *Star Trek* and *Star Wars* novels, and I had a story in a *Star Wars* anthology and *Darkover* anthologies—and I have since gone on to novel-length works in that world). I asked her if she regretted taking time from her original writing and she said that the tie-ins made it financially possible to work on other, less commercial projects. The way she discussed her work made it clear that she did her best, no matter what the story, how her imagination and sensibilities and values enriched everything she produced. That has stayed with me over the years as I've wrestled with my insane expectations of myself and my work: write the best you can with whatever life gives you. The rest will take care of itself.

Ironically, the last book Vonda was going to format for me was a collection of my *Darkover* short fiction. Here's the last email she sent me, typically generous, loving Vonda:

> *Hi Deborah,*
> *Body is sort of setting the boundaries.*
> *I sure wish I could finish the book for you.*
> *Hugs, V.*

So of course the book is dedicated to her. Miss you much, my dear friend. 𝒱

Nancy Jane Moore
Memories of Vonda

I KNEW VONDA N. MCINTYRE THROUGH HER BOOKS long before I met her. In fact, I knew her through her work even before I became a fan who looked for everything she wrote.

In 2015, when she was guest of honor at the Worldcon in Spokane, she asked me to interview her for the program. (This was yet another example of Vonda's well-known generosity. My first novel, which she had blurbed, had just come out, and she gave me the opportunity to be noticed at the convention.) In preparation for the program, which was to focus on her work, I looked at her books to see if there was anything important I had missed, and saw her first novel, *The Exile Waiting*. I didn't remember ever reading it.

Five pages into it, I realized that not only had I read it, but it was that book that I'd been trying to find again for decades, the one where the story stuck with me even though I'd forgotten both the author and the title. I was a little embarrassed, but in my defense I first read it back when I had just started reading science fiction and had no real awareness of who the writers were. I did confess this to Vonda.

So first of all, Vonda was a brilliant writer who wrote the kind of stories that get under your skin and stay with you, the ones that matter, the ones that shape our lives and help us figure out what the world and the future are about. If she had never been anything else, that would have been more than enough. But of course, as many people can testify, she was much more than that, a generous person who helped so many others in ways large and small, without fanfare.

I first met in her person when I was at Clarion West and had my first experience of her generosity in the late 1990s when she helped me deal with electronics and SFWA. But it was when we started Book View Café in 2008 that I really got to know her.

Book View Café is a publishing co-op run by its authors. When we started it, Vonda did three important things. She joined, she asked Ursula K. Le Guin to become a member, and, when we began publishing e-books, she published all of her backlist plus some new stories exclusively on Book View Café.

All of that would have been enough. Her presence along with that of Ursula gave the co-op credibility. But of course, Vonda did much more. She formatted people's e-books. She worked to make the bookstore function properly. She helped with the technical side of the blog. She even did a lot of copy editing and proofreading as well as doing the required review of books that weren't reprints.

I got to know Vonda because she edited some of my work, formatted my books, and helped me out with the blog. That professional friendship blossomed into more of a personal one, and I visited her in Seattle on several occasions. She always took time to make sure I saw something wonderful about her city. We shared our experiences with aikido.

In the summer of 2018, she asked me to do a beta read on the novel she'd just finished. It is, as you might expect, a *tour de force*. I cannot wait to see it in print. I was so glad she made the effort to do a final round of revisions before she died.

Since she had let me see her book, I got up the nerve to ask her to look at the one I finished last year. Her advice made the book better. I was looking forward to more experiences like that.

Since we didn't live in the same place, most of our friendship came through email. It always gave me a spark of joy when I saw I had a message from her, even if it was about some problem at Book View Café. We had a lot of exchanges about spam comments on the blog and provided support to each other in the wake of the political debacle in the U.S. casual exchanges, but that's how you keep up friendships across distances.

I do not have enough words to express how much I miss those emails.

Perhaps the hardest thing about getting older is the loss of other people. And of those losses, the very worst is that of people who were taken from us too soon. That's how I feel about Vonda. *V*

Nancy Jane Moore interviews Vonda at the 2015 WorldCon.
Photo by Leslie Howle.

Beaded Sea-Creatures

Julie E. Coryell
Colorful Crocheted Critters and Creations

I HAVE BEEN MEANING TO CONTRIBUTE the story underlying Vonda's prolific colorful crocheted critters and creations: founder and director (Australian) Margaret Wertheim, the Institute of Figuring, 2003; this non-profit, Los Angeles-based organization "promotes the public understanding of the poetic and aesthetic dimensions of science, mathematics and the technical arts."

I learned about and joined the institute about 2007–10 for the crocheted coral reef project, and learned then about hyperbolic geometry and the craft of mathematician Daina Taimina who figured out how to crochet models. All in the context of feminine craft and discovery. For me this is a powerful expression of Vonda's mind and life: learning, creating, playing on the unfurling leading edges of physics, mathematics, arts, materials, the riot of colors, shapes, textures of her crocheted creations. It is consoling to keep learning of Vonda's reach into so many hearts. With gratitude for the great circle of caring that celebrates and enlivens our memories of her.

When I was a co-founder of the Women Studies program at the University of Washington in 1970–71, Susan Rubinyi-Anderson sought me out, joining my spouse, Seelye Martin's nudging at home, to form a course on women and science fiction. She introduced me to Vonda, and Vonda brought along

Ursula K. Le Guin. Soon after, Susan and Vonda collaborated on the anthology, *Aurora: Beyond Equality*.

We met intermittently. We had a son, and Vonda enjoyed going out to dinner with us, particularly at the Taiwanese wok restaurant in her neighborhood. She, like many Chinese families, enjoyed the company of children. Vonda joined the Seattle school of aikido, founded by Mary Heiny 1976–86, and still going. We had a daughter and life became more complicated. In 1984, I mentioned to Vonda that I desired to organize my address book and she invited me to come to her sunroom study where she would teach me database entry on her squat barely portable Compaq computer. Taking refuge under her wing was a welcome break for me. We must have taken two-three months of afternoon sessions. Then she offered to pioneer formatting the file with the help of her downstairs apartment-mate to print said book on 5" x 8" Rediform blank pages. Carolyn and Vonda are still in my book!

I bless Vonda's name for her personal tutorial on use of the computer, her appreciation of the significance of an address book as a memory palace, and her generous gifts of time, space, and attention to a mother of two young children. (I think she would have liked these two germinal books: Jonathan Spence, *The Memory Palace of Matteo Ricci*, 1984, and Angela Garbes, *Like a Mother*, 2018). ∇

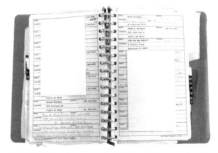

In 1984, Vonda gave Julie Coryell some basic computer training and helped her set up a vital tool—her address book.
Photo by Julie E. Coryell.

Ctein
Expanding upon Vonda's Legacy...

WHAT VONDA CALLED "BEADED SEA CREATURES" were more than just amusements and lovely art (I'm happy and honored to own one). Vonda's work was part of a discipline variously called "mathematical knitting" and "crochet topology."

I can't explain how this works in any detail, for the simple reason that I don't knit or crochet, but the gist of it is that many mathematical descriptions of topological surfaces can be transformed into a set of instructions for knitting or crocheting or doing beadwork. It's a wonderful way to instantiate surfaces that are very difficult to visualize from their equations.

It's a serious subset of the field of topology and Vonda's work in this area has been cited in academic publications.

Sea Creature by Vonda, given to Donna Haraway.
Photo by Donna Haraway.

ALL OF MY HUMAN AND NONHUMAN COMPANIONS join me in sending you every kind of energy for finishing your project! The beaded beings in my life are especially insistent that I send back to you their lust for entangled well-being, especially in hard times. I attach a picture of your gift to me that it may resonate its energies back to you. Along the way, I added a lemon from our tree. My condolences to all of Vonda's family and friends. Her writing mattered to me for decades, and then her beaded jellies for the crochet coral reef brought us together personally. May her whimsical and gorgeous beaded critters strengthen Vonda's world in the rich multispecies complexities that sustained her for such a rich and generous life.

Donna Haraway

I COORDINATEd or otherwise supported Potlatch charity auctions for the last six or so years. Vonda was always a willing contributor of her amazing beaded sea creatures and books to support the auction. With her last contribution, she graciously added an extra for me to keep as my very own. I greatly appreciated this as I was always outbid during the auctions. I used to attend her annual holiday party in the 1980's with a group of Bay Area fans and will always recall her graciousness as the host for these events. Not much I know, but I will always treasure my memories of Vonda and her books.

Karen Dawn Plaskon

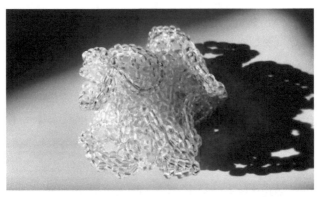

Sea creature by Vonda, given to Stephanie A. Smith. Photo by Stephanie A. Smith.

Marine flatworms by Vonda.

THANK YOU FOr sharing your beautiful bead work (especially the glowing Octopuses), the tips about hyperbolic crochet techniques and of course your unique wordsmith abilities, which will delight and educate countless curious minds for years to come. Continuing to use your crochet tips in my projects to create large to medium Hyperbolic Stress Balls (crocheted very tightly) and smaller balls to attach to Twiddle (Sensitivity) Muffs for the Developmentally Disabled and Alzheimer Patients, also to make Hyperbolic-style ruffled edges for donated pet cage pads and welcome blankets for new refuge families. You are treasured and appreciated for your beautiful spirit and for generously sharing your creative talents. Thank you especially for sharing your journey with all of us.

Lynn Johanna a.k.a. Lady Willow

Memories & Legacies

Alma Alexander

YOU WERE CO-GOH at the very first science fiction convention I went to. It was in Auckland, in 1995. (The other GOH was Roger Zelazny; that was one of his last hurrahs because the con was in April and by June we had lost him...) I have to confess that the reason I raced to that con, when I found out about it, was Roger Zelazny who had been one of my literary gods for years. I had not read anything by you at that time.

But I got into the writing workshop that the two GOHs were running at the con. I remember it with astounding clarity. The format was that each of us five participants got to say a few words about the others' stories, and then you two, the pros, weighed in. Before I got my benediction from Zelazny, I received back the copy of the story that had gone to you.

My eyes crossed. You had annotated it to an inch of its life, little scribbles in pencil in every available space. Every single thing, even when I was being pulled up for some literary sin, intensely kind, and apropos, and valuable (and there were a couple of scribbles in there that merely said "nice!" so there was that... :)) I pored over that manuscript for weeks afterwards. I learned more from that one manuscript than I might have done in a year's writing course. Somehow I ended up with your email.

I knew you were in Seattle. And some little while later I found myself in Vancouver, Canada and emailed you, and said, hey, remember me? I'm the ingénue from the Auckland workshop. And I'm near(ish) to where you are. I might be coming down to Seattle for the day. Could I—um—buy you a cup of coffee or something? There was every possibility that you would look at that email and go, who the heck is this and why is she emailing me?

Instead, you emailed me back, and told me that there seemed to be little point in breaking my neck whiplashing between Vancouver and Seattle for a couple of hours, that there was a party at your place that night (hello Vanguard!), and that I could come to that and crash on your couch that night. You picked me up when I got to Seattle and you said, mysteriously, that you wanted to show me something before you took me home. I said, what? and you said, just keep your eyes peeled. That is how I met the Fremont Troll, gasping as he first hove into view, and you wore...such a smile.

Then it was home, and party, and you introduced me to your friends, and in the aftermath you and I stood at your kitchen sink washing dishes and having a companionable discussion about science fiction, writing, life, and everything. I have never forgotten this. I never will.

I've been re-reading some of your books. *Dreamsnake*, of course, and then there was something that I'd forgotten that I owned—signed by you—at that Auckland con, so many years ago: *Enterprise: Captain Kirk's First Adventure*. I'm lingering over the last pages of that right now.

Back in Auckland in 1995 you were an unknown to me. But I discovered you, then. And I kept on discovering you. And the unknown writer became a vibrant, kind, smart, passionate person—one whom I have been proud and happy to know.

Thank you for the words. And the dishes at midnight. And the Troll.

The dream was easy to interpret. The night after Vonda died, I dealt with my grief at her passing in my usual way—I went to sleep, and my subconscious presented me with a dream. I shared it on Facebook:

My dreams have always been a place of mystery and wonder and every so often they hand me something wrapped in dream-stuff that is very very easy to "interpret."

I dreamed that I was in this place—airy and open, very simple, open beams, stuff like that, it almost looked like a place where one might spend a week or two on a holiday rather than a permanent residence—and there were other people there too, it was pretty crowded, there was food put out, it was clearly a gathering of some sort. I recognized faces—Jane Hawkins, Kate Schaefer, Amy Thomson…they were all trying to tell me that we need to go, that we need to be somewhere, and I was reluctant, and dragging my feet, and saying, give me just a bit more time.

Finally I followed them all out, onto a landing from which you had to climb up to another landing before you could climb down and exit the structure. Then we're all standing on this undulating stretch of sand dunes covered with sparse golden grass and there is a hint of sun glittering on open sea a bit further off—but the light, the light is that of an early spring morning, brittle and bright and sharp, just at that moment when everything gets a defined shadow…except that it was also muted, translucent, misty, like a finger-smudged pastel drawing, and nothing had a sharp edge to it at all.

Somebody who was wearing some sort of loose artist smock with huge pockets reached into one of the pockets and brought out this little green circular...something...and then put it on the ground at their feet, and the circle unwound and became this tiny green snake, and the snake slipped into the grass and the sand and the mist and disappeared...and I could see, far enough away for the face to be unclear, a figure with short dandelion white hair, waiting, and then the figure turned, and walked away.

I know who that figure was. I know where the little snake was going.

Vonda McIntyre left us the story...but the dreamsnake went with her, into the morning. 𝒱

Vonda was one of the 32+ returning guests of honor who attended WisCon 30 in May 2006. Photo by Mary Langenfeld.

Gary L. Benson
How I Discovered my Portrait of Vonda

I WALKED UP TO HER HOME, not knowing what to expect. It was the mid 1980's and I was assigned to photograph a local SF author named Vonda N. McIntyre. I was starting out as an editorial photographer and I knew I had to find something good.

When she opened the door, I was not sure if she was interested to have her portrait taken, as she seemed a bit shy with a "I'm not that excited about having my portrait taken today" vibe. Not to be dissuaded, I tried a few places outside but nothing seemed to be working. I wondered if I would find a good portrait of her after all.

She shared with me about her writing and how rewarding it was, but with times of frustration as any creative endeavor can be in trying to make a living. We went back inside and I noticed the soft light coming through her picture window; I said to her, "sit here on your couch and think about your writing... your next project." It was then that I knew I'd tapped into her soul, as she had the look in her eyes of creativity, wonder and amazement in what she loved to do—write. It was as though I wasn't there—only an observer of her in deep thought. I knew then that I had my image.

When Vonda saw it published, she knew it too. She used my portrait on many of her books, and after that we became friends. I will always remember and be thankful for the oppor-

tunity I had back then to be in her world for a short time...
even when at first she was not excited to have me there...but in
the end, I was able to find a portrait that revealed the essence
of who she was. 𝒱

Photo by Gary L. Benson, who writes, "I clearly remember that day I went to her house to take her portrait; it has always been one of my favorites."

NOT A SURPRISE, of course, but a real loss. *Dreamsnake* in particular is a treasure.

Liz Carey

GOODBYE, VONDA. I hope those who weren't able to share with you what you or your work meant to them, will now share those thoughts with others.

Frank Catalano

I REMEMBER JANE AND VONDA'S HOUSEWARMING PARTY in 1978, which was also a surprise thirtieth birthday party for Susan Wood and Vonda (their birthdays were a week apart). To get the cake (which had both their names) set up in the living room, devious Jane got Susan to keep Vonda busy, and Vonda to keep Susan busy. When they came into the room—double gotcha!

Eli Cohen

Frances Collin
Three Memories

Frances Collin is Vonda's agent.

WELCOME TO SEATTLE!: there was a con, I don't remember where, with Ursula the guest of honor. Vonda was there. We all three had dinner together at least once. Vonda, Ursula and I clinked glasses, and they both intoned "welcome to Seattle." I soon found out it was their custom when they found themselves together in other places…[and] this was delicious: on the Saturday, several writers were in a large room at a long table, and fans were permitted to bring their books for signing. The line of fans waiting for Ursula to sign their books went around the whole room, outside the door, and for all I know down any stairs and outside the building. On Sunday, Ursula turned her name tag to the blank side and wrote "She who doesn't sign books on Sunday."

Unless I missed something, no one has mentioned Vonda's micro needle-point. She sent me a marvelous tiny rug and tinier couch pillow for the doll house I worked at building immediately after my husband died in 1977. A few years before, she had asked what my astrological sign is. I told her and launched into something about astrology, only to be told when she sent the full-size pillow she made for my birthday that year, the sign itself wasn't the point, it was for the pillow.

In 1977 or thereabout New York suffered one of its many power outages on a hot, hot summer day. Vonda subsequently sent me a large metal convertible oil/electric lamp—the kind of thing one would need in a rural cabin—because she said she did not like thinking of me stuck in my apartment without enough light to read by. That was Vonda—always cutting to the heart of the matter, and generously, thoughtfully finding a way to make it better. 𝒱

Photo from Spokane Public Library.

Jack Dann

MY PAL VONDA N. MCINTYRE has just passed away. We met in 1975 at a UCLA madcap gig hosted by Harlan Ellison called Ten Tuesdays Down a Rabbit Hole. He invited a bunch of young writers to LA to do shtick over a weekend. Young Turks such as Vonda, Gardner Dozois, Lisa Tuttle, George Alec Effinger, George R.R. Martin, Joe Haldeman, and Ed Bryant were there. And many others! Although Vonda and I didn't see each other much over the long years, we had bonded during a late night radio gig that Harlan had set up for us. And whooboy could Vonda write! It was only yesterday that we were writers. We were going to change the world…when the world was green. Goodbye pal. Dammit, goodbye. Rest in peace, kiddo, and if there's a hereafter, I'm sure you'll be shaking up those complacent angels and aeons or whatever the hell might be up there. 𝒱

THERE MAY HAVE BEEN CUSSING. There may still be cussing. I will miss her and remember her, her strength and her compassion and understanding and…damn.

Doctor Science

IT WAS A GREAT HONOR to be able to care for Vonda and provide support for Jane (Hawkins) and Kate (Schaefer) during Vonda's last days. Vonda's kindness to me as a new Seattleite decades ago will not be forgotten; I am grateful to have been able to give back just a little bit.

Ellen Eades

SHE MADE A GREAT IMPRESSION on my young mind and I will never forget her.

Anthony Evans

BEST WISHES TO A WONDERFUL LADY. Your stories and your kindness have both made my life better.

Deb Geisler

SHE WAS A JOY AND A PLEASURE to have as our guest as at Sasquan. I will not forget her. Vonda, on whatever starry road you travel, I'd be proud to walk with you…it was, for me, a light in a time of darkness.

Glenn Glazer

VERY SAD NEWS. I've enjoyed her work for years and years.

William Grabowski

I HAVE BEEN A FAN and follower of Vonda's work since *Dreamsnake* came out and it charged my love for biology with the triploidy reproduction for the snakes. Incredible concept. I am so sad that you are going through this journey but wanted you to know that you have many long time fans sending support and prayers. I will always treasure my signed copy of *Dreamsnake*.

Susan Gray

Eileen Gunn
A Remembrance of Vonda N. McIntyre

Originally published in *Locus Magazine*, May 2019.

VONDA MCINTYRE WROTE SO BRILLIANTLY, accomplished so much, and did so many good, secret things that it's hard to write about her without making her sound like a thirty-foot tall, winged figure clothed in white samite and brandishing a sword. In real life, she was a smallish, quiet-spoken person, self-effacing unless she got her dander up, who wore comfortable clothing in jewel colors. She usually kept her sword sheathed at her side, and her wings were never in evidence until she unsheathed the sword. She once confided to me that Ursula K. Le Guin was a wolverine when defending her friends; Vonda had that same loyalty and fierceness in defense of others, especially women, and in response to perceived injustice of any kind.

For a writer of such scope and power, Vonda seemed, at first glance, to be a reticent, even shy person. She was quiet and private; she had opinions, but she often didn't state them unless provoked. Asked whether she was actively trying to be subversive when she wrote *Dreamsnake*, she admitted that, in writing, "a lot of that stuff happens in your brain before you're really conscious of it," and she was good at channeling anger and frustration into ground-breaking fiction about women, about gender issues, about the personal cost of human inhumanity. She was wise about the process of writing, about the way a writer's subconscious can bring brilliance to her work. In addition to reading her fiction, we should read the essays she wrote and the interviews that she did over the years: they make it clear that she knew how to free her mind to let it create, and yet, in retrospect, she knew exactly what she had done and meant every word.

Right now, I am reading Vonda's new, as-yet-unpublished novel, *The Curve of the World,* on my iPhone. It's a wonderful, luminous story, and in reading it, the quotidian falls away and it becomes a wide-ranging exploration of the origin of ideas and the birth of civilization. As many people know, Vonda had been working on it for well over a decade, and she finished it through an effort of will. She had less than two months of life left after being diagnosed with pancreatic cancer, a disease that is often discovered only when it's too late. She didn't drop everything and go to places she loved and wanted to revisit; she stayed home. Under the direction of her friends Jane Hawkins and Kate Schaefer, whose organizational skills could launch a successful invasion of Russia, a team of Vonda's friends took care of her needs and gave her time and privacy. She finished her book.

I think writers sometimes fear, when in the middle of an important work, that they could die before completing it. As in so many other matters, Vonda showed us, with grace and courage, how to do the right thing. Thank you, Vonda. *V*

Fonda Lee

I DISCOVERED VONDA'S WORK as a teen, reading her novelizations of the *Star Trek II, III,* and *IV* movies. As a *Star Trek* fan at a young age, those books were a gateway into a lifelong passion for science fiction stories, motivating me to seek out the works of Isaac Asimov, Ray Bradbury, Anne McCaffrey, as well as Vonda's other work.

Vonda was immensely generous and supportive to new writers. I met her in person for the first time at WorldCon in 2015 where she was the Guest of Honor. I was a debut novelist and was excited and intimidated to be on a panel with a writer I'd admired since I was young. When I introduced myself, "Hi, I'm Fonda," she said, "Hi Fonda, I'm Vonda." We both laughed and after the panel, she invited me to breakfast the following morning. It was one of the highlights of my WorldCon.

We kept up occasional correspondence over the following years and I had the pleasure of being invited to stay with Vonda when I visited Seattle (she remembered early career writers being short on funds!). I considered her a personal role model: a talented, whip-smart, hard-working author, a woman who had left an indelible mark on the field of speculative fiction but who never ceased to be unfailingly humble and kind.

I write action-adventure science fiction stories, and I once confessed that I'd considered whether I ought to write under a male or gender neutral pseudonym. I decided I didn't want to obscure my gender, regardless of potential prejudice. Vonda's reaction to me was blunt, "Don't do it." She was rightfully proud of the strides that authors like her friend Ursula K. LeGuin and she had made in proving women to be a force in the field of speculative fiction. She was working on her final book up until the end of her life. I wanted to be like Vonda, and I still do.

I JUST WANTED TO SAY that I really loved your *Star Wars* book *The Crystal Star*…it was one of the first *Star Wars* expanded universe books I ever had when I was a child and it was also one of my favorites. Thank you so much for writing it; it truly captured my imagination and inspired me.

JLH

Vonda and Eileen Gunn. Photo by Nancy Kress.

Leslie Howle
Vonda N. McIntyre, Writer, Artist, and "Mother of Writers"

Originally published in *Locus Magazine*, May 2019.

I HAD JUST GRADUATED from the University of Washington when I read *Dreamsnake* by Vonda N. McIntyre. I was so moved by the story that when I heard that Vonda lived in Seattle, I looked her up in the White Pages and called her.

"Is this Vonda McIntyre?" I asked.

"Yes," she said.

"The Vonda N. McIntyre? The woman who wrote *Dreamsnake?*"

She laughed. "Last time I checked that was me," she said.

Vonda's kindly, amused reaction led to a conversation that was the beginning of a long, life-changing friendship. Because I told Vonda I was writing fiction, she told me about the Clarion West workshop. I applied, and was accepted as a student to the class of 1985. I later learned that Vonda brought Clarion West to Seattle after graduating from the original Clarion workshop in Pennsylvania in 1970, where she and Octavia Butler were classmates. This remarkable woman took on the task of running Clarion West by herself for three years; all while attending graduate school in genetics at the University of Washington. When she finally had to surrender to give up running the workshop, Clarion West lay dormant until it was revived over a decade later by J.T. Stewart and Marilyn Holt at Seattle Central Community College in 1984.

Because of Vonda, when J.T. and Marilyn couldn't continue running the workshop anymore after my class of '85, I was one of a handful of graduates from the classes of '84 and '85 who stepped up to help rebuild Clarion West as a 501(c)3 nonprofit, and eventually ended up working as an administrator. Because of Vonda, I found myself investing a chunk of my adult life to helping build the Clarion West workshop and community into the sustainable organization it is today. My work as CW administrator and workshop director was always inspired and supported by Vonda. Did Vonda McIntyre have an impact on my life? I'll say she did!

Vonda was always there for me with advice, inspiration, problem solving, and a shoulder to lean on. She was like a fairy godmother to Clarion West. When CW needed a new office for our archives, she let us use the downstairs of her house. She helped with fund raising and was always happy to come talk to CW students as a "mystery muse" guest speaker. Every year she presented each of them with one of her lovely hand-crocheted "sea creatures." She was kind and encouraging to new writers and always made time for them.

Vonda was a strong, iconic woman, a trailblazer for women science fiction writers. At the time *Dreamsnake* won the Nebula award, she was only the second woman to ever win. She was the third woman to win the Hugo award for best novel. She was influenced early on by writers Joanna Russ and Ursula K. Le Guin and became a trailblazer in a male-dominated genre. Vonda was an inspiring writer and artist, and I will always remember her talent, intelligence, wry humor, generosity, and many kindnesses. I am deeply grateful for the good times we shared and wish we could have had just one more catch-up lunch at her favorite local Indian restaurant. My heart is full with love and memories.

It hurt my heart when I visited Vonda the day before she passed away, but she looked beautiful and seemed at peace. Now she is gone, fleeting snapshots of memories come to mind, like a dinner at my house where Vonda and Octavia Butler had us in stitches with funny stories about their summer at the Clarion workshop in 1970; or the early '80's *Star Trek* media event in Seattle where Vonda was introduced on a dark stage standing in a circle of light looking as if she had just "beamed aboard." A second later, George Takei, the actor who played Sulu on *Star Trek*, "beamed aboard" next to her. I'll never forget the look on Vonda's face when he leaned over from his circle of light to kiss her on the cheek; she turned so red! It was Vonda who gave Mr. Sulu the first name of Hikaru in her book *The Entropy Effect*, and it was obvious that George liked and respected Vonda.

I am delighted that she was able to complete her last novel, *The Curve of the World*, and look forward to reading it. I heard a rumor that they might release the film version of her novel *The Moon and the Sun* before the end of the year. It would be a fitting tribute to see the film on the big screen at last, but sad that she couldn't be there to enjoy watching it in a theatre with her friends.

I will miss our lunches at the Indian restaurant and long conversations about writing, good books, science, and life. Warm thanks, gratitude, and hugs to Vonda's awesome posse of friends who took turns caring for Vonda at home, especially Jane Hawkins, Kate Schaefer, and a score of others. She had a steady stream of loving friends by her side during her last days; it was beautiful. Her voice has gone silent, and the world is a poorer place. I miss her already. It's comforting to imagine her hanging out with her good friends Ursula K. Le Guin and Octavia Butler right now; it makes me smile. I looked up to all three of these brilliant, wise and wonderful women and feel blessed by their friendship. They are gone, but they will always live in my heart. *V*

THANK YOU VONDA for all the wonderful stories you gave us. When we met at Norwescon back in the '80s, I knew I had a great friend. We lost contact till Worldcon in Spokane. And when we met up again. It was like yesterday that we saw each other. You will be missed but you will always be with us as you left a mark in each and every one of us who had the pleasure of knowing you. Rest sweet Vonda. *V*

Kevin Kuenkler

VONDA WAS ALSO ONE OF THE GUESTS OF HONOR at the 1990 Westercon, which I co-chaired. She was a delightful person, and I will miss her a lot. *V*

John Lorentz

The Second Annual Science Fiction Ladies Lunch at Nancy Kress' apartment in Seattle. Photo by Nancy Kress.

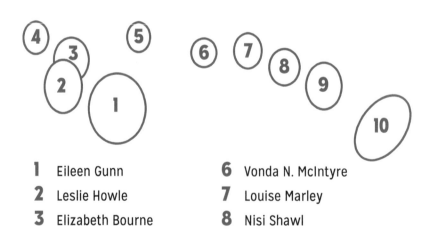

1 Eileen Gunn
2 Leslie Howle
3 Elizabeth Bourne
4 Janet Freeman-Daily
5 Brenda Cooper
6 Vonda N. McIntyre
7 Louise Marley
8 Nisi Shawl
9 Kelly Eskridge
10 Nicola Griffith

Kate MacDonald

Kate MacDonald is editor of Handheld Press

I FIRST ENCOUNTERED VONDA'S WRITING when I was working at Aberdeen's science fiction bookshop in the early 1980's. The owner wanted his Saturday afternoons off when Aberdeen Football Club was playing at home, so I was the Saturday girl for home matches when the city emptied its male population into *Pittodrie* football stadium.

The shop was quiet, so I was looking through the bookshelves to see what new stock had arrived in the week, and spotted two books with gorgeous cover art: the Pan editions of *Dreamsnake* and *The Exile Waiting*. I bought them both (I probably got staff discount on their 75p cover price), read them one after the other, and entered a new world. This was the first time I had read feminist science fiction and recognized it for what it was. Later, I found a U.S. edition of *Fireflood and Other Stories*, and devoured that too.

Scroll forward thirty-five years. I wasn't a *Star Trek* fan or interested in *Star Wars* novelizations, so I didn't realize until very recently that Vonda had written a great deal more than her first three books, but it didn't matter; I was a devoted fan on that basis alone.

I discovered the Book View Café in 2015 when I wrote a profile about it for *Vulpes Libris* and contacted Vonda, with some trepidation, by email to arrange this. I experienced some residual fangirliness, but she was straightforward and friendly, and that sent me back to her novels again (I still had them, but my daughters weren't interested in SF, only fantasy). I decided to teach "Of Mist and Grass and Sand" in a university module on gender and disability, sending my students to the BVC to buy their copies. I posted reviews of *Dreamsnake* and *Exile* on my personal website, and then in late 2018, when I had been a publisher for eighteen months, it dawned on me that I could republish *The Exile Waiting*. It seemed to be out of print, and I didn't see any publicity for it on the Gollancz site, which had already reissued *Dreamsnake* in their SF Masterworks series.

Exile wasn't on my republishing wishlist for our Handheld Classics list, but it was suddenly blindingly obvious that I should try for the rights. It would also be our first classic where the author was still alive, as Vonda was still very active as a novelist and publisher in her own right. I emailed Vonda and her agent Fran (Collin) over Christmas and New Year 2018, and I signed the contract in January 2019. Vonda and I had several good email conversations talking through my editing process, and her requirements as the author, and we agreed that I would use her master copy of the text, and would ask permission for every alteration, down to comma placement.

In February Vonda told me that she had received a diagnosis of cancer, and that she wasn't expected to live for more than a year. That was a punch to the stomach, as now Vonda would very likely not be alive when *Exile* was republished, after all. So I decided to bring publication forward from spring 2020, when I had planned to bring *Exile* out as a 45th Anniversa-

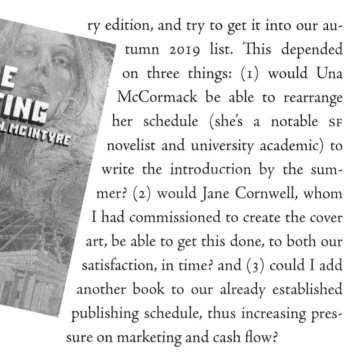

ry edition, and try to get it into our autumn 2019 list. This depended on three things: (1) would Una McCormack be able to rearrange her schedule (she's a notable SF novelist and university academic) to write the introduction by the summer? (2) would Jane Cornwell, whom I had commissioned to create the cover art, be able to get this done, to both our satisfaction, in time? and (3) could I add another book to our already established publishing schedule, thus increasing pressure on marketing and cash flow?

Handheld had just taken on a freelance marketing manager, so that would avoid the stress I'd put myself under in late 2018, when I'd added a title at the last minute and was not happy with how we presented it because I was overloaded. I moved a book scheduled for 2019 (a second collection of fantasy short stories by Sylvia Townsend Warner; she didn't mind) back into 2020, making room for *Exile* in the printing budget. Una was able to shuffle her work around and will be sending me the introduction in summer 2019, making an October 2019 publication possible. Jane went at the digital painting full steam ahead, and we agreed the final cover artwork in mid March. Our designer Nadja created the cover in half a day. Vonda emailed me on 25 March that she thought it looked great. She died some days later.

We're still going to publish in October, because the book deserves to come out as soon as possible. I also want to launch it at the UK's Fantasycon and Bristolcon, where many of Vonda's fans will be happy to see it, and we can present her original vision of Center and the world of *Dreamsnake* to a new generation of readers. I am particularly grateful to the women (all women, as it happens: this was a no-fuss all-female effort) whose generosity and willingness to adapt to the new timescale made it possible for Vonda to see the cover, and to know that *Exile* was on its way back. 𝒱

I KNEW VONDA BACK IN THE DAYS of early Norwescons, when we were both young and starting out. I love her books and am so sorry I lost touch with her. Good bye, Vonda, I'll treasure the memories of you. 𝒱

Sharan Newman

Vonda demonstrates a beading technique to Kate Yule, 2006, at WisCon 30. Photo by Elisabeth Vonarburg.

Paul Preuss
Goodbye to Vonda

Originally published in *Locus Magazine*, May 2019.

I MET VONDA WHILE WANDERING around the 1979 Westercon in San Francisco, my first-ever science fiction convention. The name on her badge was one of the few I recognized, but not because *Dreamsnake* was in the midst of its Nebula/Locus/Hugo award sweep, of which I was oblivious. I said something suave like, "oh, you're a friend of Ursula K. Le Guin, aren't you?" Vonda's gaze was steel: "yeah, and who are you?" which was how I learned that she wasted no time on fools.

A mumbled explanation relieved the tension (Ursula had recently dissected my first attempt at a novel), but in those days "friending" could take time. Nevertheless I soon became familiar with Vonda's razor-sharp intellect, her multiple talents, scientific grounding, and tireless energy; we even shared some opinions, including a preference for women SF writers. Correspondence grew into a close, if intermittent, association.

In a fast-changing world Vonda was a great guide through each new technology, mastering every advance in word processing and email ("you don't really have to answer by return electron") and the flotsam later dragged in by the internet. Her most essential quality, generosity, emerged early. She shared what she valued with enthusiasm, like the time she drove half a day to show me what was left of Mount Saint Helens.

She drove for Ursula and Charles when they could no longer drive themselves to the ranch in eastern Oregon where my wife, Debra, and I met them each August during the Perseid meteor shower. Vonda, who knew every constellation and major star, got us out of the lawn chairs and into sleeping bags and comforters; flat on our backs in one of the darkest places in the U.S., we watched meteors blaze down the canyon as long as we could stay awake.

We visited Vonda this February; between the time we left California and the time we reached Seattle, she'd gotten the fatal news. Plans changed, and we had only a couple of hours with her. *The Curve of the World*, her latest manuscript, is an extraordinary adventure set in a re-imagined Bronze Age; Vonda worried about stories she'd adapted from indigenous peoples ("the stories are owned by the tellers; I don't want to use them without permission"). About *The Moon and the Sun*, a fine novel and a movie too many years in the making, she said she looked forward to seeing it no matter what they eventually name it, "even though there's almost nothing left of what I wrote."

Together we ached for our lost loved ones—Ursula, Vonda's sister Carolyn, too many others—but she didn't want to talk about what was wrong with her. She told us the details in an email the next day.

We'd hoped she would be with us for at least a year. We got a few weeks. I have lost my most supportive and encouraging writer friend. I will miss Vonda, as I miss Ursula, the woman who pointed me to her. *V*

Debbie Notkin & Laurie Toby Edison

Originally published in *Body Impolitic*, Debbie Notkin and Laurie Toby Edison's blog

VONDA NEEL MCINTYRE DIED IN HER HOME in Seattle on Monday, April 1, 2019, of pancreatic cancer. Her official obituary and her *New York Times* obituary are excellent resources for the facts of her life and death.

Vonda's writing deserves a great deal of attention and comment, as does her key role in early *Star Trek* canon creation. But we want to talk about knowing her as a friend. Both of us have separately stayed in her home, sat up with her late at night over a glass of wine, discussed life, the universe, and everything. Both of us are fans not just of the writing, and not just of the beaded sea creatures which decorate her home and the homes of so many people who knew her, but of Vonda the human being. Both of us are lonelier without her.

Laurie says:
I remember staying with Vonda in Seattle and sitting with her in her living room talking until late at night over wine. We would talk about families, life complications and sometimes about our work: in my case, about my art; in hers, about the Book View Café press and the business of writing. And very occasionally about the writing itself.

I admired her work and the way she recast our concepts of how the world could work. She was one of the feminist science fiction writers that I most admired.

I loved her sea creatures; they were stunning and superbly original. They really looked like they could swim away. I have one swimming in the air in my living room. I created a world for them by making an undersea display for her with a fish tank in a window. Her creatures swam, hid in coral and just hung in their space. I loved doing it for her. Vonda always talked about the creatures as a hobby but it was an art form. I told her that on more than one occasion, but she never agreed with me.

I made a dreamsnake pendant for the Spokane Worldcon, where Vonda was a guest of honor. She was totally delighted with it when I gave it to her during a dinner we had the last night of the convention. I had planned to make a design from *The Moon and the Sun* for this year's Wiscon, but every time I open the book, I'm too sad. It will wait until I can read and appreciate it. But it feels good to know that she would have been happy that I made it.

We didn't see each other often but she had a real place in my life and I'll miss her a lot.

Debbie says:
What stands out for me about Vonda is that she was the single most considerate person I have ever known. Every single choice that she made took into account the comfort and convenience of the folks her choice might affect. She told me several times that she wanted to have "the best guest room in the city of Seattle," and she would always ask "What could make it better?

What could make you more comfortable?" And she would really want to know the answer.

She told me once that she had been shopping for a new car, and the salesman had suggested a car with a driver's side air bag only. She was horrified. "What could be worse," she said with a shudder, "than walking away from an accident where your passenger was killed?"

In 2013, when I thought I might be spending extended time in Seattle to be at another deathbed, I planned to stay not in Vonda's perfect guest room, but in her equally perfect spare apartment downstairs. I can't begin to express how much of a relief it was to know there was a place I could stay where I wouldn't be in anyone's way, where I could fix myself breakfast, be out all night if I needed to, and have the comfort of superb company available whenever Vonda was available. The story didn't turn out that way, but the option was literally invaluable.

Just a few comments on the books:
Since we try to bring this blog back to the body when we can, it is crucial to celebrate Vonda for being the first person (perhaps anywhere ever) to write about contraception by biofeedback, in a culture where people are commonly taught and expected to be able to control their own body temperature to avoid or encourage conception. In *Dreamsnake*, she built this story through the lens of a man who is deeply ashamed of his inability to hold up his end of the social contract—and how he and the novel's protagonist solve the problem together.

Ursula Le Guin and Vonda were the very best of friends. In Le Guin's essay about *Dreamsnake*, she also notices Vonda's kindness:

> *Dreamsnake is written in a clear, quick-moving prose, with brief, lyrically intense landscape passages that take the reader straight into its half-familiar, half-strange desert world, and fine descriptions of the characters' emotional states and moods and changes. And its generosity to those characters is quite unusual…*
>
> *Yes, there is some wishful thinking in McIntyre's book, but it is so thoroughly, thoughtfully worked out in terms of social and personal behavior that its demonstration of a permanent streak of kindness in human nature is convincing—and as far from sentimentality as it is from cynicism.*

We can't think of a more fitting description of—not just *Dreamsnake*—but Vonda herself. V

Vonda on Crete, at Phasistos. Photo by Alice Lengers.

SHE WAS ONE OF THE HEARTS of our Seattle community and this loss has left many of us reeling. She was so unabashedly good and thoughtful and she knew so much that any walk with her was an amazing conversation that roved all over the place and always left you inspired. If you knew Vonda, you loved her. That was just how it was. For me, at least. I haven't seen *Captain Marvel* yet. I'm probably going to make that part of this afternoon's self-care, in memory of one of the most marvelous, strong champions of humanity I ever had the privilege of interacting with.

Cat Rambo

LUKE MCGUFF IS ORIGINALLY FROM CHICAGO, so I've known him as long as he's been in fandom. In 1990 my job sent me to a week-long technical class in Seattle. Luke was living with Jane Hawkins then, and I asked him if it was practical for them to put me up. Sure, ok. I hadn't known that Jane was housemates with Vonda. So when I met her for the first time, our conversation was about coordinating who got the shower when in the morning. (OK, *I thought it was kind of funny.*)

Neil Rest

Sigh. This hurts. A lot. Not unexpected, but still painful even so. My condolences to all who held her dear. *Requiescat In Pace.*

Robert Reynolds

Vonda and I took our first aikido class together after watching a demo at a writing workshop. She persevered, I didn't. Always regretted that, and that we lost touch. She mentored me through my first experience with an agent, and cheered me on when I finally got published. But best of all, that week of her guidance in the writing workshop instilled in me a little voice—hers, of course—reminding me never to run with the easy idea. Shine on, Starfarer.

Candace Robb

Oh, I will miss her so much. Thank you Vonda for so many hours of wonderful reading. I reread your books constantly. Rest in peace.

Robyn

I WISH GREAT STRENGTH AND THANKFULNESS to the caregivers who are there for Vonda, and of course my thoughts are with Vonda as well. I never knew her well, but we corresponded now and then, as when I asked if she could also sign a bookplate for my mother because I was presenting her with a hardcover copy of *The Moon and the Sun* for Christmas. One of my favorite novels, and I've always regretted that the movie was not released. Such an outstanding writer! When the time comes, Vonda, go gently. You will be long remembered.

Jennifer Roberson

YOU ARE IN MY THOUGHTS EVERYDAY, Vonda. You know how I've loved reading your work since I first discovered *The Exile Waiting* back in the '70s. I've recommended it to a lot of friends over the years, along with *Dreamsnake*. I felt so blessed meeting you in 2008 when you welcomed me into your home and showed me around Seattle before Clarion. I often think of all your lovely crocheted sea creatures and still have the one you gave me. Much love and gratitude, xx.

Carol Ryles

VONDA N MCINTYRE EXTRAORDINARY WRITER, powerful woman, and knitter of aliens is no longer among us. So sadness.

Geoff Ryman

The Moon and the Sun, by Vonda N. McIntyre (1997) has been made into a movie, *The King's Daughter*. It is directed by Sean McNamara with a screenplay Ronald Bass, Barry Berman, Laura Harrington, and James Schamus. The film stars Pierce Brosnan as King Louis XIV, Kaya Scodelario as Marie-Josèphe, and Benjamin Walker as Yves De La Croix. Open Road Films will release the film.

Pierce Brosnan and Vonda at filming of *The King's Daughter*, 2014. Photo by Sean McNamara.

Vonda wrote: "Between shots, Pierce Brosnan spotted me. 'Vonda, you must have a chair!'

"'Really, I'm okay—'

"'You're the author, you must have a chair.' And he found me a chair next to Sean, who agreed that I must have a chair. It was the perfect place to see the scenes as they were being shot, and the playbacks.

"When the King and God (have you seen *The Stunt Man*? If not, go thou and see it, and you'll get the reference) say you must have a chair, you get a chair."

Pamela Sargent

Introduction for a leather-bound edition of *The Moon and the Sun* published by The Easton Press in their *Masterpieces of Science Fiction* series. More info about this series can be found here at the Internet Speculative Fiction database: http://www.isfdb.org/cgi-bin/pubseries.cgi?49

VONDA N. MCINTYRE IS A WRITER who thrives on new and different challenges in her writing. Her work is of a piece while also being varied and versatile, a more difficult feat than some readers may realize. Where another writer might have been content to settle into a niche, McIntyre seems intent on striking out in untried directions, much to the reward of her readers.

Her first novel, *The Exile Waiting* (1975), was an atmospheric adventure story set on a post-apocalyptic Earth. She followed this novel with the critically praised and extremely successful *Dreamsnake* (1978), which won both the Nebula Award and the Hugo Award for best novel of the year. *Dreamsnake*, based in part on McIntyre's Nebula Award-winning novelette "Of Mist, and Grass, and Sand" (1973) and set against the same background as *The Exile Waiting*, is a novel that demonstrates the author's gifts for characterization and exploring biological themes while telling a compelling and detailed story. Snake, the protagonist of *Dreamsnake*, is a healer who uses three different genetically-altered snakes to treat the ill and also to ease the suffering of the dying. The loss of her dreamsnake, one of her essential tools, sends Snake on a quest to acquire another one of these extremely rare creatures.

One interesting detail in *Dreamsnake* (and a quality of almost all of McIntyre's writing) is that her characters are often free of the customary gender roles and restrictions. McIntyre, along with such acclaimed writers as Ursula K. Le Guin and Joanna Russ, was a pioneer in this regard, and expresses her feminist vision with subtlety. Several supporting characters in the novel appear without first being identified by gender pronouns, thus forcing readers to examine their own assumptions about such roles. Sex and gender are also integral parts of the author's biological extrapolations. (Vonda McIntyre, trained as a biologist and who did graduate work in genetics, is well equipped to write on biological themes.) Snake, who as a healer has had to develop immunities to the venom of the snakes she uses, cannot have children as a result, since her antibodies would destroy the sperm of any male partner; healers instead adopt their children, as Snake does during the course of this novel when she rescues an abused child. Another of the people she meets on her quest is a young man shamed and shunned because he is unable to control his fertility, and has unintentionally impregnated his first lover, his deep feelings of guilt are those of a person whose culture takes for granted that all children should be planned for and wanted.

With *Dreamsnake*, McIntyre established herself as one of the most important of the science fiction writers of the 1970's, following this novel with *Fireflood and Other Stories* (1979), a collection of short fiction that demonstrates the range she was to show in her later novels. With Susan Janice Rubinyi-

Anderson, she edited the groundbreaking feminist and humanist anthology *Aurora: Beyond Equality* (1976), which included important works by Marge Piercy, James Tiptree, Jr., and Dave Skal, among others.

At this point another writer might have gone on to write more stories of Snake or other such healers, and to explore even more cultures in the setting of Snake's ruined Earth, a move that probably would have resulted in a long and successful series. Instead, McIntyre, after a side venture into writing two *Star Trek* novels (a longtime fan of the series, she brought an appreciation of the characters and her own inventiveness to these books), came out with *Superluminal* (1983), a novel in which pilots of faster-than-light ships must have their hearts replaced with artificial organs if they are to survive interstellar travel. Her characteristic themes of possible biological developments, unconventional sexual preferences and partnerships, and freedom from gender constraints are part of a story centered on Laenea, a pilot; Radu Dracul, who loves Laenea but loses her after she is biologically altered; and Orca, a member of a humanoid species genetically engineered to live in the ocean who, against the custom of her people, aspires to be a pilot.

Superluminal was followed by two more *Star Trek* novels and by *Barbary* (1986), a young adult novel, before McIntyre embarked on her *Starfarers Quartet*, which includes the novels *Starfarers* (1989), *Transition* (1990), *Metaphase* (1992), and *Nautilus* (1994). This series, centered around an alien contact specialist and her colleagues aboard the interstellar vessel *Starfarer*, superficially resembles the *Star Trek* background, but her characters are complicated and extremely appealing individuals whose personal lives and struggles are as engrossing as the problems they encounter during their space expedition.

Elements common to all of Vonda McIntyre's earlier works can be found in *The Moon and the Sun* (1997), and yet this novel, her most accomplished work to date, is also a radical departure for this writer, both in its setting and in the way that she set about to write it. In 1994, as she explains in her afterword to the book, she was given a fellowship in a screenwriting workshop for playwrights and prose writers. *The Moon and the Sun* was originally written as a screenplay, but McIntyre chose to create a novel from this story at about the same time. Having in this way already departed from her usual way of writing a novel, McIntyre also chose to set her tale not in the future but in the past, in seventeenth century France at the court of Louis XIV. This period, one of the most thoroughly documented in French history, presents a daunting challenge to any novelist wanting to make use of it; the amount of research required is immense if one is to capture the details accurately and convincingly. (I am no expert here, but have read about this historical period, one of my favorites, at length in both French and English and have visited Versailles; as far as I'm concerned, McIntyre has depicted the time and setting beautifully.) In fact by the time I reached the end of *The Moon and the Sun*, the author had so seamlessly woven together the various threads of her novel that I could not imagine her story being set anywhere else.

The Moon and the Sun is both an alternate history and a story of first contact with an alien species. That its author has also set it at a time when prevailing superstitious ways of thinking were giving way to a new spirit of scientific inquiry also makes this book a true novel of science fiction. The central characters, Marie-Josèphe de la Croix and her brother, the Jesuit scholar Yves de la Croix, embody the dawning scientific spirit of a new age. At the beginning of the novel Yves is in command of an expedition to find the legendary sea monsters rumored about in the tales of sailors; he manages to capture two, a male who dies during the capture and a female creature who survives.

The natural philosopher Yves cannot view the humanoid sea creatures as anything but beasts without souls (in this he is appropriately Cartesian). Louis XIV, "the Sun King," the powerful and extravagant monarch of France, views the sea creatures from a more credulous and superstitious perspective, as being a possible source of immortality for himself by means of an organ such creatures may possess. Marie-Josèphe, a student of mathematics who has only recently left the repressive confines of a convent to become an attendant of the wife and daughter of the King's brother at court, is prepared to assist her brother Yves in the dissection of the dead sea creature and in observing the surviving one, who clings to a precarious existence in the waters of one of the fountains of Versailles. Appropriately, it is Marie-Josèphe, a gifted and scientifically curious young woman who can be seen as a bridge between an older world view and a more enlightened culture, who first realizes that the imprisoned sea creature may be more than a soulless animal, and who first manages to communicate with it.

The scenes in which Yves performs his dissections before an audience of the King and his court while Marie-Josèphe records her brother's work by means of sketches are suspenseful and filled with realistic detail. Marie-Josèphe is a believable young woman who is both convincingly of her time (she is devout and, thanks to a childhood in the colony of Martinique and years spent in convents, a *naif* in a dissolute and sophisticated court) and a harbinger of a more scientific worldview (she has assisted Yves in some of his experiments, has taught arithmetic at the convent, and has musical talents as well). One passage in the novel captures something of Marie-Josèphe's character:

> *The morning delighted her. The world delighted her. When she kicked a small stone down the path, she thought, with a few strokes of my pen, with a calculation, I can describe the motion of its rise and fall. I can predict its effect on the next stone, and the next. M. Newton's discoveries allow me to describe anything I wish, even the future paths of the stars and the planets. And now that I am free of the convent, no one will forbid me to do so.* [p. 45]

Perhaps because this novel was originally envisioned as a screenplay, the writing is extremely visual without being overly burdened with extraneous descriptions, as though the author were skillfully using the lens of her mind's eye like a camera, focusing on exactly what is necessary. One example of McIntyre's subtlety occurs in her depiction of Lucien de Barenton, Count de Chrétien, a trusted advisor to Louis XIV who befriends Marie-Josèphe and eventually comes to love her. When he first appears, McIntyre accurately describes him as Marie-Josèphe sees him, yet without ever labeling him explicitly with the term many would use to describe someone with his particular physical disfigurement; as in her earlier works, where readers were led to confront their assumptions about gender. Count Lucien also makes us consider our assumptions and prejudices about the physical appearance of others, in particular a character filling the role here of a romantic hero. (In an interesting touch, McIntyre makes Lucien even more of an outsider and independent mind by depicting him as an atheist, a status that he finds considerably safer than being a Protestant in the court of a King dominated by his rigidly Catholic morganatic wife, Madame de Maintenon.) Her gift for dealing sympathetically with unconventional people and relationships brings depth to her portrait of the homosexual Monsieur, Duke d'Orléans and brother of the King, a figure generally treated in histories and documents as frivolous and contemptible.

McIntyre's characters, both major and minor, live and breathe on the page. As Marie-Josèphe increasingly becomes aware that the captured sea monster is another intelligent being and a member of an endangered race, she must find the will to defy her King, her Pope (Innocent III arrives at Versailles not long after the sea creature's capture), and even her own brother if she is to save the captive's life. Her motivations and feelings are complex and true to this period; she is moved not only to save the sea creature, but also the immortal soul of Louis XIV, whom she believes will be forever damned if he allows the creature to be killed and served at a lavish banquet planned for his court. In being able to understand the sea creature's true nature, a move that forces Marie-Josèphe to jettison some of her culture's deepest assumptions, she embodies a new spirit of a new age of scientific inquiry, but her growing realization of the truth about this strange being and the risks that she must take to save it threaten to condemn the young woman to the punishment of permanent confinement in a convent and the end of all her inquiries.

The Moon and the Sun was honored with the Nebula Award for best novel of 1997, but this book also won acclaim from such writers as Jean M. Auel, Ursula K. Le Guin, Paul Preuss, and Diana Gabaldon, who called it a story "balanced perfectly on the edge between enchantment and belief." This novel, engrossing as it is, still offers no clue as to what kind of novel its author will write next; but based on the evidence of *The Moon and the Sun* and Vonda N. McIntyre's past career, we can safely assume that her next work will be as well worth reading and as rewarding as this one. 𝒱

Collage by Harriet Beeman. Harriet knew Vonda through the Le Guin family and has been lifelong friends with Caroline Le Guin.

Kate Schaefer

VONDA WAS MY FRIEND FOR FORTY YEARS. We were young women together, Vonda and Jane and I and several others, and we always thought we'd be old women together, because all our parents lived into their eighties, so shouldn't we live into our eighties as well? shouldn't we? couldn't we?

I bought a house in this neighborhood because it was just a block away from the house Vonda shared with Jane Hawkins. Later, Jane and Vonda bought the house next door to the house they already had; eventually, Jane moved into the house next door, and some time after that, my stepdaughter and granddaughter moved into the space where Jane had lived, downstairs from Vonda.

Our lives were always entangled. Vonda was at my wedding to Glenn. She saw my grandchildren as infants; they're all of them voting adults now. My family stayed in her guest room. We went camping together; we bought land together, and put some small buildings on the land so we wouldn't have to sleep in tents. The land was a clear-cut when we bought it. We hired people to plant trees on it, and Vonda took chocolate chip cookies to the tree-planting crew. Twenty-eight years later, those trees are pretty tall now.

We walked together and talked about our families, about dealing with parental illness and death. She hugged me when my sister got cancer, and rejoiced with me over her recovery. I hugged her when her sister got cancer; I cried with her when her sister died. She was with us through some of the worst times of our lives and some of the best. She was part of the oxygen of my life.

What I wrote the night she died: my dear friend died this evening. Tomorrow morning I'll get up and I'll take a walk without her. We always walked on Tuesday mornings, only we haven't been walking because she's been ill. She isn't ill any more, so why can't she take a walk with me?

My gut doesn't understand anything my brain has been telling it for weeks.

And two weeks later, I wrote: our houses are full of each other's work and gifts. I hold down piles of paper with her beaded sea creatures, which make the most delightful paperweights possible. I drink tea from a cup she brought back from a trip to Thermopolis several years ago. I put my feet on a footstool she covered for me nearly thirty years ago, and try to remember the difference between crewelwork and needlepoint, because one of those is what she did and the other one isn't. Her books are on my shelves, the ones she wrote, the ones she recommended, the ones she lent me. Her old silk shirts are in my sewing supplies; I'll use them to line hats and small bags. There's a pair of suede pants in my closet. She wore them for a while before deciding they just weren't her. I wore them a few times, then decided that suede pants are just too hot. Sure, they're sexy hot, but they're also physically hot, and Seattle isn't cold enough for them.

Downstairs at her house, every window is covered with curtains I made. Her awards sit on shiny fabric I brought over.

There are flowers in a vase I gave her years ago. Her favorite vest was one I made for her, featuring embroidery stitched by another of her friends, her very closest friend. It hangs in the closet next to a velvet jacket I made her. There's a leather jacket tossed on her bed; I relined it just a few weeks ago. She never wore it outside the house.

In her last few weeks, when she could still get dressed, she usually wore shirts that had belonged to her sister. We didn't talk about why she did that. Now, I wear one of her shirts most days.

It's another Tuesday today, and I'll take a walk without her. I'll never take another walk with her. I am sure that I will reach a point where Tuesday is no longer the worst day. Maybe Tuesday will be the day when I just think about all the years of kindness and friendship; Tuesday will be the day of good memories.

Memories are completely portable, and they'll be with me as I walk, but I'll walk alone. *V*

Vonda near the Duckabush River on the Olympic Peninsula, visiting a property that was owned by Vonda, Kate Schaefer and Glenn Hackney. Vonda considered Duckabush a magical retreat, a place to find peace and heal one's soul. Photo by Stacey Vilas.

Nisi Shawl
Tribute

Originally published in *The Seattle Times*, April 9, 2019

AWARD-WINNING SEATTLE SCIENCE FICTION AUTHOR and behind-the-scenes powerhouse Vonda Neel McIntyre died in her Wallingford home on April 1, 2019. This was a little under eight weeks after her diagnosis of pancreatic cancer on February 7. Fifty-three days. That's not much time to prepare to die; McIntyre spent most of the rest of her life revising her final novel, *Curve of the World*, a book as gorgeously imaginative as her 1997 Nebula winner *The Moon and the Sun*, or her 1979 Nebula and Hugo winner *Dreamsnake*. She also managed to purchase dozens of boxes of Girl Scout cookies and donate them to the Family Works Foodbank and complete a few other generous, Vonda-like tasks.

Vonda-and-Jane Girl Scout Project, March 2019. Vonda wrote on Twitter: "When you're coming home from getting holes stuck in your side, a fun project is a good thing to look forward to.... We decided it would be fun to go buy a lot of Girl Scout Cookies and donate them to FamilyWorks Family Resource Center & Food Banks. And it was! What great kids and parents." Photo by Jane Hawkins.

Eight weeks is not much time to prepare yourself for a friend, colleague, and mentor's death, either, but McIntyre's various communities rallied 'round. Clarion West alumna and longtime volunteer Jane Hawkins put a series of schedules together: first for escorts for McIntyre's shopping expeditions, then for the solitary running of her errands, and finally for a round-the-clock bedside watch. Each schedule sparked jealous competition for available slots. We graduates and staff of the Clarion West writers workshop, which McIntyre founded in 1971, shared news of her deteriorating health with each other online; members of Pacific Northwest science fiction fandom, which for decades held parties in McIntyre's home, offered each other necessary mutual sympathy.

The sympathy was and is necessary because we've lost so much. McIntyre was at the forefront of the feminist science fiction movement of the 1970's. Like her friend and collaborator Ursula K. Le Guin (the two created several chapbooks and Christmas cards together), she challenged the unacknowledged sexism rampant at that time in literature in general and science fiction in particular. Stories by Le Guin, Joanna Russ, and other feminists included in the 1976 anthology *Aurora: Beyond Equality*, which McIntyre co-edited, envision a world free from gender bias. With the success of *Aurora* and her own writing, she inspired hundreds of other classics of the field, such as Pamela Sargent's *Women of Wonder* series. She made a difference in what sort of stories were available in the '70s and '80s, and in who could reasonably expect to write and sell them.

Today's strongly surging wave of women and non-binary people writing speculative fiction owe McIntyre a debt—and not just because of her efforts to broaden inclusion within the genre in decades past. More recently, she built and ran websites for many of these authors. She organized and administered Book View Café, a publishing cooperative with decidedly feminist members. To the very end of her short, illustrious life, she donated money in support of feminist and other social justice causes: the James Tiptree, Jr. literary awards; the Octavia E. Butler scholarship fund (she was Octavia's Clarion classmate); the ACLU; Planned Parenthood.

And many others. In the wake of McIntyre's death, anecdotes are surfacing which reveal more and more shining facets of the gem she was. Often these facets surprise her admirers. Those who knew her mainly as the author of five *Star Trek* novels are not automatically aware of the beautifully beaded sea creatures she crocheted; not all those who received these sea creatures as gifts realize their importance to the mathematical field of topology. Two women who belonged to McIntyre's "posse"—the extensive circle of friends who kept her company, took her to her last doctor appointments and bought her last ginger beers—will assemble into a book many of these highly personal stories of joke *krugerrands* and toenail trimming sessions and other gloriously insiderish specificities. Hopefully these slices of life will be holographic: though flat themselves, they'll give a three-dimensional sense of the depths McIntyre contained. Quite a few who'll read this have contributed to it, Jeanne Gomoll and Stephanie A. Smith's print-on-demand book. All of us should read *Remembering Vonda* as soon as it becomes available—watch for a posting on the topic at her CaringBridge site, https://www.caringbridge.org/visit/VondanMcIntyre. We should also make a point of reading and rereading every Vonda N. McIntyre story and novel we can find. What else can we do to commemorate the life of our founding fairy godmother? We can write our best, as she would have wished. We can support each other, as she would have wished. 𝒱

Vonda, Suzy McKee Charnas, Nancy Jane Moore, and Jim Lutz at the 2016 Tiptree Symposium in Eugene, OR.

DEAREST VONDA: My mother gave me *Dreamsnake* for Christmas waaaaay back in the 1980's...it has always stayed with me as a beautiful and moving story, and an exceptional blend of SF and fantasy. Since then I've had the good fortune to enjoy other tales of your making. Your great gift of story-telling became a lovely gift to me. I thank you for using your skills, for all the work you put into honing your talents, and your ability to imagine...it is no small thing to be able to entertain and move and stimulate the imaginations of others. It is sacred. While this leg of your journey is coming to a close, another door and another adventure will surely open for you. My good wishes and heartfelt thanks go with you wherever you travel, Storyteller. xx.

Sylvi Shayl

Vonda at Sasquan, 2015. Photo by Shannon Page.

ON MAY 20TH, 1980, I called Vonda. When she answered, I said "Hi, Vonda. How's your ash?" Without a pause, she said "Volcano jokes are getting very old around here, Jon." And we laughed, and went on from there. (It had been just barely two days since what was probably the largest eruption in U.S. history.) Jokes? What jokes?? She was so sharp... sigh. Most of the time I spent hanging out with Vonda wasn't of that sort. She showed me her copy of Chocolate Decadence; we went out to dinner various times—she introduced me to *Bizarro* and several other cool restaurants in Wallingford; I lived in her parents' house in Bellevue for a while; that sort of thing. Vonda and her mom gave me the little electric kiln that her mom had used a bunch of years earlier. It was my first kiln. Later I converted it, and it became my first gas kiln; but that's more about me than it is about her.

Jon Singer

Jon Singer
Chocolate Decadence (as modified by Vonda N. McIntyre)

LINE THE BOTTOM OF AN EIGHT-INCH ROUND CAKE PAN with parchment or with buttered, floured waxed paper.

In a double boiler, melt one pound of dark sweet chocolate and five ounces (not Tbs) of butter. Mix together, remove from heat, let rest.

Put four eggs and one Tablespoon sugar in the top of a double boiler or a bain-marie. Whisk continuously till sugar dissolves and mixture darkens (it doesn't, much) and becomes barely warm.

Remove quickly from heat and beat at high speed with electric mixer till eggs reach "their potential treble volume and are the consistency of lightly whipped cream." (Recipe says ten minutes. Half that suffices. This can be done with an eggbeater if you feel energetic.)

Fold in one Tablespoon flour. (This is not a typo.)

Mix 1/3 of the egg mixture into the chocolate mixture.

Fold the chocolate mixture into the rest of the egg mixture.

Pour mixture into pan, tap pan lightly on table, put in oven.

Recipe says to cook for fifteen minutes at 425 degrees. My experience is that this is a sure way to burn it. I cook it at 350 and use my judgment on when to take it out—twenty or twenty-five minutes, more or less. Better to have chocolate sludge than chocolate brick, which is what decadence turns into when overcooked.

When it has cooled, wrap and put in freezer at least overnight. Will keep up to a month. Freezing seems to be an essential part of the recipe.

Thaw it. (It's best at room temperature; the center should have a consistency halfway between that of brownies and that of fudge.) Serve with whipped cream and/or raspberry puree. (Rum or cognac is good in the puree). 𝒱

Vonda at Sasquan, 2015. Photo by Shannon Page.

V

I GOT TO MEET MS. VONDA at my place of employment, when I worked at the library. I was introduced by a fellow co-worker. She and I had our picture taken, and had a fifteen minute discussion about writing. She was a great writer, and one of my inspirations to begin writing. R.I.P. Ms. Vonda…you will be sorely missed. *V*

Pam Smith

Vonda and Bret Smith. Photo provided by Bret Smith.

Stephanie A. Smith
The Best Guacamole Ever
(which Vonda made for the 1981 Haystackers)

INGREDIENTS

Two to four or more ripe avocados (depending on how many people you are making it for)

Lemon juice to keep said avocados from turning too brown

Garlic, minced to taste

Your favorite hot salsa (mine is either homemade or Green Mountain Gringo Hot)

Cumin, coriander powder, chili powder, and black pepper, to taste

Mayo (I use light these days)

Fresh cilantro, chopped

Peel and pulverize the avocados so that you have a thick paste; sprinkle with lemon juice. Add mayo and salsa to taste; add other spices to taste, and finally, add the cilantro. Let marinate for like twenty minutes in fridge, then sample and adjust for flavor. Don't forget the corn chips. I still prefer *Green Mountain Gringo Strips* if you can find them. 𝒱

Stephanie A. Smith
Avgolemono: For When You Aren't Feeling Well

2–3 cups chicken broth; boil
Put in some rice and boil till rice is soft
    (or use leftover rice)
Cool
Beat two eggs
Stir in
Heat gently and stir
Add lemon juice to taste
Don't boil
Serve hot or cold. 𝒱

Vonda's house. Art by Jeanne Gomoll.

A GENTLE PASSAGE INTO THE LIGHT FOR YOU, Vonda! Yesterday evening, I suddenly had a strong sense of Vonda passing, and lit a candle for her on my outdoor shrine. Then later I read the news here that she had died. Her spirit is strong!

Sara Stamey

ENDURING STRENGTH, GRACE, AND COMFORT to all those friends and loved ones who cared for Vonda, and to all her readers who admired her so. She used her many gifts and powers for good, and as a reader I am so very grateful that she did. Thank you!

Sheree Renée Thomas

I'VE KNOWN vonda since 1979. Being able to help when she needed me was a blessing, after all she has done for me. I miss her very much.

Tamara Vining

THANK YOU ALL SO MUCH for all that you've done for Vonda, and for keeping the community informed. May her memory be a blessing.

Donna J. Wagner

Cynthia Ward
Goodbye, Vonda

SHE IS KNOWN AS AN EXCELLENT AND IMPORTANT WRITER of science fiction, and as the writer of *Star Trek* and *Star Wars* novels who gave Hikaru Sulu his first name. What is not well known, because she did not draw attention to herself, is what a pioneer she was. In speculative fiction and in life, she was a feminist. In electronic publishing, she was on the board of early e-book publisher Fictionwise, and she founded the publishing cooperative Book View Café. She became web-master (an unpaid position) for the Science Fiction and Fantasy Writers of America in the early days of the web and created many SFWA members' websites. She co-founded the Clarion West writers' workshop.

She was always warm and gracious to Clarion West students, and I would be unsurprised to learn she quietly met and talked with everyone who ever attended the workshop since its launch. She was also gracious to anyone else she encountered at the workshops, as my friend Michele Kerr can verify regarding our discussion of *Dreamsnake's* Merideth with Vonda. I gave her champagne to thank her for my and WTO's websites, but not enough. She refused to let Amy Wolf and me buy her lunch at the Sasquan World Science Fiction convention in 2015, insisting on paying, though she didn't know me very well, and though it was she who was the convention guest of honor and deserved the paid dinner. I never had the opportunity to pay Vonda back with a meal, and I should have given her more champagne. Far more. 𝒱

Vonda wearing a shirt that was a gift from her sister Carolyn. Carolyn bought the fabric and a seamstress sewed the patchwork shirts to Carolyn's direction. Photo by Stacey Vilas.

Tom Whitmore
Remembering Vonda

Originally published in *Locus Magazine*, May 2019.

I FIRST MET VONDA AFTER ST. LOUISCON IN 1969—at least, that's the way I remember it. I know we got into a correspondence while I was still in high school, and she was a graduate student at the University of Washington. We'd write each other up to three letters in a week. We stopped writing regularly when she went off to Clarion, but we stayed in touch when I visited Seattle, and since I moved here. She's one of my oldest friends in the SF community.

Vonda was intensely private. Everyone will tell you this. They may not tell you that she was almost always the smartest person in the room, in part because she had absolutely no need to let other people know this. Her humor (often self-deprecating) frequently had insights that didn't hit for a few hours. Vonda was deep, and Vonda was kind. She had very little use for fools; but that just means she didn't spend time with them. And the best stories about her require time, and context, because the stories were always deeper than a summary would show.

She avoided the spotlight. She'd probably be embarrassed at what everyone is saying about her. And what we're all saying is just a tiny bit of who she was, what she did, and how much she supported her friends and colleagues. I don't think I'll ever know how much of a hole her death leaves; I don't think I can even see how much of a personal hole is there right now. I know that I'll remember her, and try to live in a way that would make her proud that she knew me.

Graham Watt
Remembering Vonda N. McIntyre

I MET VONDA N. MCINTYRE AT MISCON 4, May 1989 in Missoula, Montana. This was the con which was kicked out of their hotel on the first night. Since I arrived in the dead of night and slept in my car, I found this out the next morning. Dead...I could have died before I got the chance to meet her. Since I had driven from Olympia, Washington to attend the con after being up all night, I was exhausted, alone, and pushing to keep going. I fell asleep at the wheel doing 70 mph in a graceful sweeping curve on I-90 somewhere halfway across Idaho. I woke as the right corner of the car touched the guardrail. I twitched the steering hard left, scraped twin lines across the side of the car, and spun out in the middle of the banked curve, ending up perpendicular with the car blocking two lanes. Alive.

Instead of just stopping, which anyone with common sense would have done, I continued on, stupidly, risking it all and others around me. Hours later, I eventually made it to hotel. Parked on the street and climbed in to the back of the car to sleep at last.

Waking well after noon, I talked with someone who gave me directions to the house where they were attempting to salvage the con. They successfully did that.

Lawncon 1(what I called it) went on. Gaming, vendors, filk musicians, and even the costume contest carried on. Vonda N.

McIntyre was on site, accepted books for autographs, met people, and she even judged the costume masquerade. I still have my paperback of *Barbary* which she signed. I asked for and took a photo of her at her judging table. I include it here. I shot 1 roll of color and 1 roll of b/w film at this event. Her portrait shows her friendly grace and power. I recall she was wearing black leather zip up boots, similar to those of *Star Trek* the original series. She was super gracious. Later on, when Usenet was starting, I found her email address and exchanged a note. She had her basement of books. I remember her explaining that selling the signed author copies were an important source of funds. Her books and her presence at Miscon 4 left lasting impressions in my memory. She lives on. 𝒱

Vonda McIntyre at the MISCON 4 costume judging table, May 1989 in Missoula Montana. Photo by Graham Watt

THE RACE IS NOT OVER THE RACE GOES ON. She was a great author in a time where women were second fiddle in the genre.

Eric Williams

VONDA, YOU ARE NOT JUST A GREAT WRITER, you are one of the most truly decent people I've been lucky enough to know. I think the first thing of yours I read was *The Entropy Effect*, and I went on to read many more. Best always to you and those close to you.

Chris Willrich

Amy Wolf
In Memoriam: R.I.P., Vonda N. McIntyre, author, mentor, friend

I FIRST MET VONDA AT CLARION WEST '92, but we didn't become good friends until she attended a script workshop in L.A. and stayed at my place. Vonda was the perfect guest, even buying me a coffee grinder as a thank you gift. I think it's because she said that *angelenos* make their coffee so you can read a newspaper through it.

Later, when I moved to Seattle, Vonda and I would get together at least once a month to dine at the fabulous Judy Foo's *Snappy Dragon*. During our outings, Vonda was unfailingly supportive, offering writerly and publishing advice, and what was much more important, an aura of calm severely missing from my life.

We called each other "Arnie" and "Vinnie" since we thought that male non-de-plums would "help" us in Hollywood. Over the course of thirty years, we bonded over films, writing, and eggrolls.

Vonda was my best friend in Seattle: the only one I saw regularly in the flesh. Her passing creates a void that I can never fill. The abruptness of her departure, the way she was torn from us in a single month, is the most difficult thing I have ever had to face—and I'm a two-time cancer survivor. I cherish the time I got to spend by her bedside, threatening to read *War and Peace* if she misbehaved.

Farewell, Vinnie. May your next travels span the universe. Thanks for listening to all my kvetching, and most of all, laughing at my jokes. All of us who had the privilege of knowing Vonda can truly say, without embellishment, that her memory will serve as our ultimate blessing. *Vale, mi amica.* 𝒱

Amy Wolf and Vonda McIntyre at Spokane World Con in 2015. Photo provided by Amy Wolf.

DESPITE WORKING on behalf of her amazing books for close to fifteen years, Vonda and I never met in person. However, over the course of our conversations via email, she would often mention things she loved, so I will always associate Vonda with the Winter Solstice, her fondness for vibrant purple flowers, her beautiful and intricate bead creatures, and her anecdotes about the natural world when she stayed at the yurt. It has been an honor to play a part in representing her work in the marketplace.

Sara Yake
Frances Collin Literary Agency

(Left to right) Chelsea Quinn Yarbro, Tappan King, Beth Meacham, and Vonda at the 1979 Worldcon in Brighton England. Photo provided by Beth Meacham.

Interviews

Paul Novitski
Vonda McIntyre

Originally published in Starship, *spring 1979.*

VONDA N. MCINTYRE SOLD HER FIRST SCIENCE FICTION STORY in 1969. Since then her steady rise in popularity among readers and editors alike is easily explainable: her prose possesses a grace and power which grip the reader, gently but firmly, from first page to last. She moves people with words.

Vonda attended the Clarion Science Fiction Writers' Workshop in 1970, the last year that workshop was held in Clarion, Pennsylvania. The next three years in a row she tackled the mammoth task of organizing Clarion West at the University of Washington. On the fourth year she rested, preferring to nurture the remnants of her sanity in peace and quiet. In 1973 she won the Nebula Award for her novelette, "Of Mist, and Grass, and Sand." By 1975 her first novel appeared, entitled *The Exile Waiting*.

Her most recent[1] novel *Dreamsnake* utilizes "Of Mist, and Grass, and Sand" as its opening chapter. It was published last year by Houghton Mifflin. *Aztecs*, a novella, one of the most beautiful pieces of fiction she has written, ran in competition for the Nebula this spring. Forthcoming is "Elfleda," described by one reader as an erotic hard-science fantasy; it will be pub-

---

1   Subsequent to this Interview McIntyre wrote and published fifteen books.

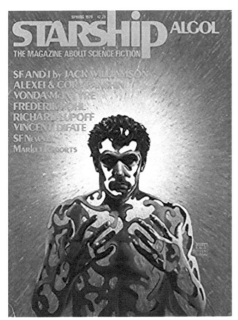

Starship #34, Spring 1979, containing Paul Novitski's interview with Vonda N. McIntyre. Starship was published by Andrew Porter. With this issue *Algol* changed its name to *Starship*.

lished as a chapbook with color illustrations by Pendragon Press.

Vonda lives in a small house on the shore of Lake Washington in Seattle. Until recently housemates with an orange cat, she now shares her home with a plesiosaur. This interview was conducted on a sunny afternoon in May over several small bottles of fruit juice. The mood was a deep and quiet blue.

Novitski: When did fiction writing become your vocation?

McIntyre: Well, it was either immediately before or immediately after I quit graduate school, because I haven't had a regular job since then. I did the whole thing with editing the literary magazine in high school and all that, and I sold a couple of stories when I was a senior in college. I'd sold about five or six by the time I left graduate school, when I realized that as a grad student I made a terrific SF writer. One of the reasons I quit school was that I didn't have time to write the novel I was working on.

Novitski: That was *The Exile Waiting*?

McIntyre: Yes. I'd been working on that for a long time. It took me an amazingly long time to write.

Novitski: What aspects of your childhood contributed to your desire to write?

McIntyre: I've been reading science fiction all my life; I don't remember learning to read, so I sort of grew up with it. I was your typical science fiction fan when I was a kid. I read a lot, I was pretty much of a loner. When I realized that real people wrote science fiction, I wanted to do it, too. My dad is really a good writer, though he doesn't do it professionally.

Novitski: In several of your stories and in *Dreamsnake*, horses figure largely, and I know that you own a horse yourself.

McIntyre: Oh yes, I was a horse freak when I was a kid. My horse is retired now, but I do still have him. By the time I finished *Dreamsnake* I was beginning to get a little worried that I'd really written a space opera without replacing the horses with rocket ships. [Laughs] but I liked it so I left it that way.

Novitski: What are your writing habits?

McIntyre: I work late at night. In the daytime I sort of wander around going, "where's the mail? I want my mail." I'm a real mailbox vampire. I hover around it till it comes. They've just switched the schedules around, so now it doesn't come till 2:30, and makes me crazy. I mean, you wake up at nine o'clock in the morning and you think, god, it's five hours before the mail comes, what's the point? It does not take five hours to drink your first cup of coffee.

I compose in longhand. I felt a little guilty about that for a long time, but I finally decided I was wasting a lot of energy feeling guilty about the way I write. The people who compose on the typewriter feel that it's unprofessional to handwrite their manuscripts. They will give you big lectures about it, lay guilt-trips on you. But I find that in typing I cut a lot, and rewrite, and generally retype it several times. So my handwritten drafts don't even count as first drafts, they're sort of zeroth drafts. The first draft is when I get it into type: I write all over the typescript and type it again, and I may write all over that typescript and type that again. I think it results in cleaner prose, because you cannot write purple prose and not notice it that way. I have a tendency to get a little florid occasionally and when I look at it again, I go, "oh, god, did I really do that? I can't stand it!" whereas I know people who go straight from the head to the printed version. They type it and that's it. I think most of them would be better writers if they went through at least one draft.

Novitski: Your latest novel, *Dreamsnake*, was published by Houghton Mifflin, who have never published any science fiction to speak of. What do you think accounts for this?

McIntyre: My agent sent it to them, they read it, and they liked it. I guess it was just due to my agent's nerve, and the fact that she had worked with Houghton Mifflin before and thought they might like *Dreamsnake*.

They did publish Tolkien, you know. I have a feeling that must have taken a certain amount of willingness to publish something unusual. They publish Tom Robbins, who is not your basic staid, mainstream writer. I don't think they have any plans to get into science fiction in a big way, but I certainly never felt like a second-class writer, somebody they took on just because "that sci-fi stuff" is popular. I thought they bought *Dreamsnake* because they thought it was a good book and they liked it.

But the cover of *Dreamsnake* doesn't say "science fiction." I think it mentions science fiction on the top line of the inside dust-jacket flap in the back... here it is, "one of a growing number of SF novels..." but Houghton Mifflin usually doesn't publish science fiction; the book doesn't say, "Houghton Mifflin science fiction" because there's no such line.

Novitski: And you think it might sell better for that reason?

McIntyre: I don't know if it will or not. Science fiction tends to sell slowly but steadily. Whether my book will have anywhere near the success of some of the underground best-sellers—which is how science fiction becomes a bestseller, by going "underground," like *Dune*—I don't know. If it does fairly well, maybe Houghton Mifflin will publish more science fiction.

Novitski: Hypothetically, do you think that, say, if Hugo Gernsback had been run over by a truck when he was a young boy and had never started publishing pulp science fiction and therefore it had never become a set genre as it is now... do you think that if you were writing fiction, and if the writers you emulated were the same ones you like best now—Kate Wilhelm and Samuel R. Delany and so on—and they were writing similar things to what they are in this universe, do you think that...where am I?

McIntyre: I know what you're asking. There's a difference between the way science fiction is perceived in England versus the way it's perceived in the states. That difference is that we have had to fight our way out of the pulp tradition. The pulp tradition took over from the literary tradition of science fiction in this country. We have Hugo Gernsback and John W. Campbell to look on as literary progenitors, whereas British science fiction writers have H.G. Wells—

Novitski:—Olaf Stapledon—

McIntyre:—And George Orwell, people like that. So I think that if Hugo Gernsback had been run over by a truck it might not have been a bad thing. [Laughs] God forbid I should wish retroactive death on anybody. But if he'd published *Popular Mechanics* instead, we might not have gotten mired in that whole how-many-words-can-you-pad-the-story-out-to business. And we might not have had to go through the whole new wave/old wave fight which was a waste of a large number of people's energies. But I like publishing in the science fiction magazines. More people read your stuff if you publish in the magazines, and that's the whole idea. I'm glad they're there. On the other hand, before the pulps came along, science fiction was published in the major slicks. On the other hand—and if you're a science fiction writer you can have three—the slick magazine fiction market is essentially dead. The mainstream short fiction market is almost non-existent. A short story writer, unless they're a science fiction writer, has almost no place to publish. A lot of places won't even read unsolicited manuscripts. Esquire won't any more, hasn't for a couple of years. The college magazines, the little magazines, the literary magazines will, but you can't exist—you can do a lot of talking about art for art's sake, and support yourself either in a garret somewhere or in a cushy university position, which is what most people who write for literary magazines do. But you can't exist as a writer. You either starve or teach. Whereas you can make a fairly decent living as a science fiction writer.

Novitski: So the only way to live as a full-time fiction writer outside the SF field is to write novels exclusively.

McIntyre: Essentially. Those people who have a talent for short fiction are essentially lost, as far as I can see.

Novitski: There's only *Playboy*, and the *New Yorker*—

McIntyre: Yes, but *Playboy* and the *New Yorker* won't read unsolicited manuscripts. Well, maybe they'll read them, but when was the last time you heard of anyone selling a story out of the slush-piles to the *New Yorker*? I heard of somebody who got a hand-written rejection slip once, but that's about it. And he had a cover letter from Donald Barthelme!

Novitski: What other writers have influenced you?

McIntyre: There are people who have influenced me personally, and people who have influenced me professionally. I really like most of Chip Delany's work. I enjoy Roger Zelazny, and of course Ursula K. Le Guin. I think Kate Wilhelm is fantastic. But I don't really know consciously what has influenced me. I didn't set out to try to write like someone, although I can see similarities with some writers.

Novitski: Are there any writers outside SF who have impressed you a lot?

McIntyre: No, not really. I feel that is a flaw in my own background. Almost everything I read when I was a kid was science fiction, and in college the literature courses I took were classes in myth—classical mythology, Norse mythology, ancient Indic literature—but I didn't take any American or English literature, and my literature background is really flawed.

Slick magazine fiction all seems to have the same plot to me. In *Ms. Magazine*, the fiction runs to: unliberated woman goes back to college, has unhappy affair with English instructor, becomes liberated and unhappy and divorces her husband. I find that very depressing, that the characters in stories like that have to give up so much to discover their own identities. Is that what we're working for? I don't think so. I hope not.

But maybe I'm being unfair to mainstream writers. I think Marge Piercy is terrific. I find her non-science fiction as readable as her science fiction.

Novitski: By her science fiction, you're referring to *Woman on the Edge of Time?*

McIntyre: Yes, and *Dance the Eagle to Sleep*, too. But she's also written a number of other novels.

Novitski: The parts of *Woman on the Edge of Time* that took place in the present, in mental institutions, I thought were superb, but as much as I agreed with Piercy's vision I didn't think the futuristic parts were very good science fiction.

McIntyre: It's science fiction in the tradition of the utopian novel, which means it's pretty didactic. If you like utopian novels then you put up with this sort of, "now we'll show you around our wonderful new society—"

Novitski: "—And we'll tell you all about it!"

McIntyre: "—And tell you all about it," right. Perhaps it's her background in real fiction, quote-unquote. People who don't come out of the SF tradition have trouble justifying a pure science fiction novel, and that might be why she mixed the present with the future like that. Yes, the mental institution scenes were incredibly powerful.

Novitski: Do you feel an allegiance with any class of writers, say, women writers, or science fiction writers, or young writers?

McIntyre: I suppose I do, although I'm not sure I could categorize it quite that easily. I'm getting a little old to be in the class of young writers. People keep asking me to be on panels on the new writer. There was a big conference at Berkeley, u.c. Berkeley extension, and they called me up and wanted me to talk for three hours on being a new writer! [Laughs] I said, well, in the first place, if I talked for three hours you wouldn't want to hear it, and in the second place... it's like calling Gardner Dozois a new young writer. I'm almost thirty, and he was a big name in the field when I was a Clarion student. He came to Clarion and everyone went, "gosh wow, Gardner Dozois, holy shit!" and people are still calling Gardner Dozois a new young writer. I don't know what that means. When Chip Delany was at Clarion he was twenty-nine, I think, and he said something about being a little old to still be the *enfant terrible* of science fiction. On the other hand, Harlan Ellison's forty-four and he's still the *enfant terrible* of science fiction. But then...Harlan is Harlan.

A lot of the writers that I like to read are women, and most of my best friends in the writing community are other women writers, though not exclusively. For instance, one of the best writers coming up now—he's been going, what, three or four years, now—is Herb Varley. I mean, he's amazing. He's gone just straight to the top of the field. The thing that the science fiction community is going to have to answer for in the next few years is why his novel didn't get on either major award ballot. That's embarrassing! It's bad enough that it didn't get on the Hugo ballot, but for the sfwa to just sit there and go, "uhh, *Ophiuchi Hotline*, what's that?"...you could scream, you really could. I don't know what's going on in the field that he hasn't gotten more recognition, because he's just super.

I feel my allegiances are with the people I admire, the people who are good writers, who write in a humanistic tradition which we almost have to invent ourselves. There's Rosel George Brown, who—God—has been dead for fifteen years. She was just super. Her people were people, they did what they wanted to do, not what they were told they should have done because of the way they were born. Delany has done the same.

Novitski: There's Elizabeth Lynn, although a lot of her material hasn't come out yet.

McIntyre: I think she's going to follow in Herb Varley's footsteps and leap to the top of the field as soon as her books start coming out, which won't be for about another year. I've read her first novel in manuscript and I really enjoyed it. She's got several more coming out in rapid succession.

I haven't been reading a lot of fiction in the last couple of years, so there are a lot of new writers that I'm not as familiar with as I should be. I started looking up stories by people on the John W. Campbell award ballot so I could vote intelligently, and I was horrified by a couple of the names on the list. If that's the best we can do, we're in deep trouble. But Liz Lynn is on it, and that's neat. Lisa Tuttle won it a couple of years ago, which is cool. So maybe the field isn't descending into disaster quite yet.

Novitski: It seems to me that in the past five or ten years an increasing proportion of SF writers have been women, and in fact a larger percentage of the best SF writers have been women.

McIntyre: Well, in the past few years a greater percentage of every profession has been women. Everything is opening up. My own theory is that no editor with any sense will turn down a good story simply because it was written by a woman. Even a flaming misogynist who's a successful book editor is not going to turn down a good story by a woman. He may not pay her as much... but he's going to print it.

So the difficulty isn't in getting printed if you're a good writer. The difficulty is in having enough gall to start sending your stuff out to begin with. Up till recently I don't think women got as much encouragement in that direction as young male writers did. On the other hand, writing has been a field that women traditionally have been able to succeed in. That is, writing in general; maybe not science fiction in particular, which until ten or fifteen years ago was perceived as a literature for male adolescents of whatever age. But that's changing. I just think the quality of the pool from which women writers are taken tends to be a little higher to begin with because women who are mediocre never send their stuff out, whereas a lot of really mediocre guys not only send their stuff out, it gets published! [Laughs] then it gets nominated for Nebulas and Hugos.

Novitski: Has the nature of science fiction changed with the increased participation of women?

McIntyre: "Deep sigh." [Laughs] I discovered science fiction fandom in about '67 or '68. That was right after the beginning of the whole new wave phenomenon, quote-unquote, and I think that's when science fiction really started to change, with *New Worlds* and with *Dangerous Visions*.

Once the feminist movement started helping people believe that there were other options for them than what was shown as ideal in 1955, you know, the whole post-war back-to-the-kitchen business, I think that was when science fiction began to change. It wasn't so much a cause and effect as a mutual reinforcing phenomenon, where things started to change and people who wouldn't ordinarily have written science fiction saw more opportunities in the field than they might have seen before, and got interested in it. If science fiction had stayed the way it was in the fifties and early sixties, then I don't think that once I became aware of the feminist movement I would have been interested in writing science fiction. Because I wouldn't have been able to write the good old standard space opera, which is kind of fun until you realize you're totally excluded from it if you're anything but a white Anglo-Saxon/Aryan male.

Novitski: You don't think it's possible to write space opera with a black woman as the hero?

McIntyre: Oh, sure I do. For instance, I think that *Star Wars* would have been a much better picture if everybody in it hadn't been a white male, except for princess Leia who was one of the boys. But all the other women in the rebel forces are in purdah or someplace—there aren't any. By the end of *Star Wars* I was going, "yay, Darth Vader!" because at least we were allowed out on the streets in the empire. There were a couple of women in the street scenes, but in the rebel band there was princess Leia and there were guys. There weren't any women mechanics, there weren't any in that...

Novitski: In the Death Star, that space station?

McIntyre: There weren't any in the Death Star, that's true, but I mean there weren't any in the establishment on either side. There weren't any at the very end in that scene taken from that Nazi propaganda flick, where they're all standing in line … these are supposed to be rebels, and they're all standing in the orange section, and the blue section, and they're all wearing storm trooper helmets. You're sort of wondering what George Lucas is trying to tell you! You're left wondering, what's going on here, man? These are supposed to be the good guys.

I was really disappointed. I wrote a three-page letter to George Lucas and tore it up. He doesn't need some science fiction writer telling him how to improve the most successful movie ever made, but I was really disappointed. I wanted to like the film. I enjoyed much of it. You should have seen me driving up the freeway afterward—"hyper space, yaha!" I was lucky I didn't get a traffic ticket. But if he doesn't clean up his act in the sequel, then my incipient dislike of the movie is just going to burst out full force. I mean, I can see Diana Rigg as a Jedi knight. That would be sensational.

Novitski: I find it depressing that they had so much money to work with on *Star Wars* and came so close to making it a perfect movie, then blew it by being so sociologically primitive.

McIntyre: Really. I saw Carl Sagan—I'm a late-night talk-show addict—on the Johnny Carson show. Carson asked him something about *Star Wars* and Sagan said, "well, I sort of enjoyed the movie, but I thought it was very human chauvinist." He said, "I thought it was really terrible that they didn't give the Wookiee a medal at the end." And I went, "right on, Carl!" He said, "everyone in the entire universe was a white male." My God, he noticed it, that's fantastic.

Novitski: It seems apparent that not only are more women selling science fiction to editors these days, but you're being paid more than before. Do you perceive sex discrimination in SF sales today, and does it reflect in the sizes of advances?

McIntyre: I don't know that much about other people's advances. I certainly have no complaint. My career has been attended by an unbelievable amount of luck, and since the other facets of my life have not particularly been attended by a fantastic amount of luck I'm hard put to explain it, but I'm certainly not complaining.

The only quibble I have is that reprint anthologies tend heavily toward being mostly male, and that extra royalty money is what makes the difference between being a writer who does something else to support herself, and being a writer who's supported by her writing. You hear stories in which a woman will call up an editor and say, "listen, you owe me a hundred and fifty dollars and I really need it," and the editor says, "but, my dear, if you need money you should get some from your husband!" That sort of story will really put your teeth on edge. That really happened.

Novitski: Recently?

McIntyre: No, it's been several years. And it was also by an editor who's not working in the field any more, which is also encouraging. But even then, it must have been '74 or '75. There are very few people who would be quite that blatant about their discrimination today. I mean, not if they wanted to live…

Novitski: Do you think it's been an advantage for women writers that so many of the editors have been women?

McIntyre: no. I don't think it's been an advantage. You've still got to be pretty good to be published. The fact is that there are more mediocre men writers than there are mediocre women writers. There are damn few mediocre women writers who ever get published. And that's in spite of the fact that a lot of the editors in the field are women. Women are as hard on themselves as anybody. Look at all the women who are fighting to keep essentially dependent status. You can't really blame them. They're frightened of change.

I don't like change that much, which is weird for a science fiction writer to say, but it's true. The Feminist movement is not just about rights, it is about responsibilities. More responsibilities are scary. The result is that for some of the same reasons, women are as hard or harder on each other, sometimes, as men are on women or as men are on other men. Up until recently there's been no good old girl network like there's a good old boy network. Why do you think women want to get into repellent organizations like the Rotary Club or the Junior Chamber of Commerce? Because there are business contacts in them. And to say, "well, this is a men's organization, women can't be in it, they can form their own organization," is a red herring. It's to say it's only a social organization. That's baloney. Maybe technically they are social clubs, but what they're for is to give people contacts in their professions. And women need them just as much as men. Up until recently, women have had to succeed all on their own, with the result that the women who have succeeded have been super-women. Most of us aren't super-women, and I resent being told that in order to succeed I have to be one. Because I'm not.

I really admire women who can do everything. Kate Wilhelm and Ursula Le Guin are not only the best in the field but have raised families. Depending on whose family you're talking about, whether it's Kate's or Ursula's or anybody else's, you don't really know how much help they've had from husbands or whoever, but it's fairly safe to assume that most of the responsibility for the children, at least, has been with the woman. Somebody saying, "Mommy, I want a drink of water" every half hour would not make it easy to write.

Ursula says that one person cannot handle two careers successfully, be successful in both of them. But two people can handle three. And that's the way she and Charles have worked things. I think that's really a neat way of looking at it. That's obviously the ideal. How many people are privileged to be in that situation is another question.

Novitski: I believe that all fiction is political, in the sense that you can no more write apolitical fiction than you can speak without an accent. On the other hand, many artists cherish the idea that they operate outside parochial political concerns. Do you sense this conflict in yourself?

McIntyre: I'm not sure I can answer that, Paul. I know that my fiction must be political…I don't think I could write a story set in the standard universe of traditional science fiction, which is basically Middle America 1955. It would make me crazy. It makes me crazy to read stuff like that now. There's all too much of it still being published.

In one of the novellas I was trying to read by one of the people nominated for the John W. Campbell award, there was one woman mentioned—mentioned!—and she didn't even exist. Not only was she a prostitute, but she didn't even exist, she was just an excuse for this guy to leave: "I'm going to go visit this whore I know," while he was really doing something else. That was the only female person even alluded to in the whole thing. The establishment was all male, the military was all male, the rebels were all male, the underground was all male. I was reading it, going, "wha… ?" parthenogenesis? what is it?

Novitski: Clever devils, how do they breed?

McIntyre: How do they do it, yes. It was a dumb story.

Novitski: Offhand I can't remember the racial backgrounds of people in *Dreamsnake*, but weren't most of them white?

McIntyre: No. I'm not sure exactly what Arevin is, but he's at least part American Indian. And Grum's entire family is black. The people of mountainside you don't really know about, all you know is that they're very handsome people. A lot of the characters are white, that's true. I'm white. I'm middle class. An editor wanted me to change parts of "Aztecs" because she said Laenea was too WASP. And it's true, Laenea is a WASP, that's what I am. You can try to make a multiracial society and you're sort of caught between wanting to do that and not wanting to presume to know other people's experiences. And then you're balanced between a third point which is that that's what a writer's supposed to do, to accurately reflect the experiences of their characters. The whole trick is to make the characters believable.

Novitski: It's very popular these days to put a lot of different races of people into the same stories. A lot of science fiction writers are white, middle-class people, so when they do this a lot of time what they get is a lot of white, middle-class characters with different colors of skin.

McIntyre: —In clever plastic disguises, right. Yes, it's a problem. And, you know, it's not just in writing. It's one of the basic problems of our society.

Novitski: Do you think you'll do any more anthologies along the lines of *Aurora: Beyond Equality!*

McIntyre: Susan and I would like to re-edit *Aurora* now; it's been, what, five years. Writers today are caught up with the theme that we wanted to have stories written about for the anthology. It would be nice to have a bunch of humanistic science fiction stories collected in one place.

Novitski: I was one of a number of people who were criticizing *Aurora* when it came out for not containing the kind of humanistic fiction that it promised. It was an excellent anthology, but a lot of the stories in it weren't portraying equal societies, they were portraying worlds in which all the men were monsters—

McIntyre:—Or non-existent, right. I'm not ashamed of *Aurora*, I think there was some really good fiction in it, though I don't think it was completely successful in terms of what we set out to do. We didn't get any stories that were more humanistic than the ones in the book.

There was no confusion over what we would bounce and what we would buy. There was one story we bounced because it went even further than the stories that are in *Aurora* toward a female chauvinist viewpoint. It was a great story; if I'd been publishing a general interest anthology I would have bought it in a second. And half of Raccoona Sheldon's story ("Your Faces, O my Sisters, Your Faces Filled of Light!") was set in a future where either everybody of either sex calls each other "sister," or there aren't any men. But it was such an incredible story, it was just a brilliant story. We led off the anthology with it because we thought it was so good. The only thing that bothers me is that Jim Baen bought a story by Raccoona Sheldon before we did. We almost got to "discover" her, and missed by one story.

Novitski: Apparently Alice Sheldon, as James Tiptree, Jr., had been submitting stories with the Raccoona Sheldon byline for some time before that, but they never sold until "James Tiptree, Jr." started putting cover letters on them.

McIntyre: yes, but she admits that they were not her best Tiptree stories that she sent out under the Sheldon name. So I don't think you can make a case for sexual discrimination there. If you put your best stories under a male name and your second-rate stories under a female name, you can't say people are buying these because of the male name and not buying those because of the female name.

By the way, there was no cover letter from James Tiptree, Jr., on "Your Faces, O My Sisters..." in Jeff Smith's fanzine, *Khatru*, Alli Sheldon specifically excepts that story from the list of Raccoona Sheldon stories that Tiptree sponsored. It didn't have a cover letter, and it wasn't a reject Tiptree story.

Of course, we didn't know that it was James Tiptree, Jr. We got that story and we said, "we want this story! We are going to buy it." After I had corresponded with Raccoona for a while, I began to suspect that she was a creation of James Tiptree, Jr., but I didn't want to know because I liked them both. It never occurred to me that Tiptree was a creation of Raccoona Sheldon, of Alli Sheldon.

Novitski: She was using a post office box somewhere in the Midwest for Raccoona Sheldon, wasn't she?

McIntyre: Right. She was using a post office box in Florence, Wisconsin, and Tiptree's mother lived in Florence. So when we got the story from Raccoona, I wrote to Tiptree and said, "listen, I know that you want to be the unknown man of science fiction and I respect that, I promise not to pry. But if you sent Raccoona Sheldon to us, if you told her about our anthology, I really appreciate it because this is really a brilliant story, I love it." I thought it was possible that they knew each other because Florence is a small town, and they seemed to be of an age. Tiptree wrote back and said, "well, yes, we've known each other for a long time..."

I didn't pry and I've been really grateful ever since, because I could have written Raccoona and said, "hey, you know James Tiptree, Jr. tell me all about him!" and then James Tiptree, Jr.—Dr. Alice B. Sheldon—would have known that I was lying through my teeth when I promised not to pry. It was a real temptation. But after a while I really didn't want to pry because I was afraid I would find out that Raccoona Sheldon didn't exist as a person.

Novitski: You've been corresponding with Tiptree for a long time. How did you react when you found out he was a woman?

McIntyre: I sort of went, "wow... holy shit!" I was really surprised. I guess there are people going around claiming that they knew all along that Tiptree was a woman, but I have yet to see someone show me something they had in print beforehand, so I think there's a lot of revisionist history going on. It never occurred to me that Tiptree was anything but exactly what he said he was, and he was everything he said he was, except that he was a woman.

I've since got to know Alli Sheldon as Alli Sheldon. She's really a neat person and I like her a lot. The only thing I'm sorry about, in the whole situation, is that if there was one guy like Tiptree in the world, maybe there are others! [Laughs] but there wasn't a guy like Tiptree. there is a person like Alli Sheldon, and she's cool, I really like her.

Novitski: Is she different from James Tiptree, Jr.?

McIntyre: Only in that, since she's not trying to retain a pseudonym now, she doesn't have to be so cautious about what she says. She's the same person.

Novitski: What are you working on now?

McIntyre: I'm working on a kids' book. I've had a couple of ideas for short stories rolling around in my head for a long time, but I don't know what their ends are.

You put so much energy into writing a short story or even a novella. I've written two novellas and one of them just sank without a trace. It's depressing to write something that you put a lot of energy into that nobody ever gets to see, nobody ever reads. A few people saw "Aztecs," but not that many.

Novitski: That came out in Ed Bryant's anthology, *2076: The American Tricentennial*, didn't it? I never found a copy.

McIntyre: I would have been happy if the publishers had treated Ed's anthology a little better, because it had zero distribution. They were really enthusiastic about the anthology, then they published it and it just vanished. Local distributors claimed it didn't exist. That was sort of depressing.

Novitski: Will it be reprinted anywhere?

McIntyre: It's coming out in Terry Carr's *Best of the Year* anthology.

Novitski: I was dismayed that it didn't win the Nebula. Do you care very much about that award?

McIntyre: Oh, sure, it's a beautiful award. It means a lot to me. It meant a lot to me when I got the one for "Of Mist, and Grass, and Sand." Because it's your peers, essentially, who are voting for it. I've never really been in serious contention for a Hugo. It's neat if people who read your fiction like it, but it's even neater if other people in your profession like it, because they know what you go through to bring it out.

Novitski: Are you planning to make "Aztecs" into a novel?

McIntyre: Well, Radu seems to want to have some more written about him. I did sort of write myself into a corner when I said hyper-space was indescribable. You can really get yourself into a bind that way: "the indescribable monster came down the hall," and then you describe the indescribable monster for two pages. There's a certain contradiction there...

I think I'm finished with the less technological world that *Exile* and *Dreamsnake* are set in. *Aztecs* was set in an entirely different alternate future. There are still things to look at there.

Novitski: Since *The Exile Waiting* and *Dreamsnake* take place on the same world, I'm curious which took place before the other.

McIntyre: [laughs] I never figured that out. I kept trying to figure out which one came first, and I never did.

Novitski: If you ever wrote another novel set on that world, and they published it as a trilogy, you know, a boxed set, then they could label each one as the sequel to the other two.

McIntyre: The first circular trilogy!

Novitski: Both "Aztecs" and *Dreamsnake* contained hard scientific fact, precisely but as background, not foreground. In *Aztecs* the technology of interstellar spaceflight and the biological alterations of the pilots are there, but implicitly—it's where the real story begins, it isn't the whole point of the telling. Why do you choose to introduce your scientific knowledge in such a subtle fashion?

McIntyre: Because expository lumps are boring. "Hello, George, how are you today?"—"Oh, I'm fine, Fred, even though we are orbiting in our space station at 18,000 miles above the surface of the earth and running out of oxygen and our orbit is decaying, but of course you know all that." Boring!

Novitski: There isn't a dearth of technical information in your fiction—

McIntyre: No, but I try to sneak it in.

Novitski: A lot of the science fiction you grew up reading was typified by that sort of thing.

McIntyre: I was a kid, what did I know? [Laughs] we all change. Science fiction changes, and people change. That stuff was really interesting when I was a kid, that's how I got interested in science. I thought I was going to be a scientist. But I discovered after a year and a half as an apprentice scientist that what I really was was a science fiction writer.

I find science fiction that deals with people to be more interesting than science fiction that deals with gadgets, with mechanical or biological technology. My background is in genetics, so most of the technology that I deal with is biological. (I've been looking for an astronomy course for troglodytes for years, and I have yet to find it.) I just think it's more elegant to get it in sneakily, and to try not to just throw in a couple of pages of your latest physics or genetics work.

Novitski: There's also people-science. *Dreamsnake* was an example of sociological extrapolation.

McIntyre: Yes, but it wasn't based on anybody's theory, except that I snitched some of John Holt's ideas about children's rights.

Novitski: I see a greater emphasis on sociological and interpersonal relationship extrapolation in science fiction these days.

McIntyre: Yes, you're right, but that's what fiction always has been, in its ideal. It doesn't have anything to do with sociology, it has to do with fiction. See, somebody in the 1930's didn't say,

"Freud has all these interesting theories and I think I'll write a novel on that." They said, "I have all these characters that I want to write a novel about." Science fiction has just recently progressed to that stage, where it's the people who are important, rather than, "look at the neat robot I just invented." "Look at the neat robot I just invented" is entertaining and interesting and fun sometimes, but it's not the only thing that science fiction can do.

Novitski: I remember that you once cited three stages in the evolution of science fiction—

McIntyre: I think either Joanna Russ or Chip Delany made those up. The first stage is, "look at the neat robot I just invented." The second stage is, "look at the neat things that my robot can do." And the third stage is, "look at the effect the robot has on the people and the society that it was invented in," which is more complicated.

Novitski: And you're interested in writing just third stage science fiction.

McIntyre: Basically, yes. I've invented things that I thought were neat, but they were inventions that needed people. The people were more important than the inventions, even though the inventions had an effect on the people.

I could have written a story in which a couple of biofeedback researchers stood around and talked about a method of birth control by biofeedback, but I don't think that would have been very interesting.

Novitski: Oh, right—you accomplish the same end in *Dreamsnake*, except—

McIntyre: —Except that it's a given of the society. Everybody can do it, unless they're really screwed up, as Gabriel was.

Novitski: And since it's second nature to them, they use it sometimes in the novel but they usually don't talk about it.

McIntyre: Right.

Novitski: As contrasted, say, with *Rendezvous with Rama*, in which a huge spaceship enters our solar system with no aliens on it at all, no reflection of the society or psychology of the people who used it, just the hardware. That kind of science fiction still has a big following.

McIntyre: Well, it's fun to read. People's inventions are interesting, but not as a steady diet. You want a little variety. No, there were things that bugged me about *Rendezvous with Rama*, but I thought the hardware was very interesting. The characters weren't very interesting, unfortunately.

Novitski: Kate Wilhelm has spoken on the subject of the sweet-and-savage novels being published these days. These books, often written by men under female bylines, deal with masochism and rape, the social and sexual powerlessness of women. According to the editors who buy these books—themselves women—these books sell large to a female audience. What do you think is the appeal of these novels, and how do they fit into our current stage of literary and political history?

McIntyre: [laughs]

Novitski: In twenty-five words or less?

McIntyre: Well, they don't appeal to me, so I don't know what the appeal of them is. In case you haven't noticed, there's a big backlash going on in this country. There's a whole neo-puritanical movement on, there's the reverse discrimination, there's the anti-gay rights, there's the anti-practically everybody's rights, except middle class white WASPS who do it in the missionary position with nobody but their legal spouse. I mean, it's really scary. I don't know how far back this one is going to go, but I hope it stops pretty soon. I don't like to think of the fellow citizens of the country that I'm a citizen of as being such incredible bigots. I find it really upsetting. That's one of the reasons I write science fiction. [Laughs] I can't stand the real world.

Novitski: So science fiction is an escape literature for you?

McIntyre: You 'betcha.

T. Jackson King
SFCInterviews: Vonda N. McIntyre

Originally published in *Science Fiction Chronicle*, 1993

TWENTY-THREE YEARS AS A WRITER gives you some perspective.

For Nebula and Hugo Award-winning novelist Vonda N. McIntyre, it's taught her a number of things. About Hollywood. About social justice. About a career in writing. And especially about the craft of writing, and whether it can be taught.

"I think innate talent is the least of it. I don't think writing can be taught—I think you have to teach yourself. I think a workshop or a writing 'teacher' can give people the opportunity to learn to write. But you can't pour it into somebody's ear. It's hard work."

Quite so. But McIntyre has served as a writer in residence at Clarion West twice—in 1984 and 1990—and was a student at the original Clarion workshop in Pennsylvania, in 1970. Still, her advice for new writers doesn't fall into the "how-to" format: "One thing a lot of new writers don't understand, when it comes to getting published, is that half the fight is persistence. Getting a reject slip does not mean your story is bad or unpublishable. It means, as reject slips usually say, that the story doesn't fit the needs of the publication. That can mean anything. 'The magazine's full till 1996.' 'My slush pile is sixteen feet high so I'm sending everything back without reading it.' Yes, it could mean the editor hates your story. So what? It just means your taste and that particular editor's taste don't coincide. Don't put the story in the bottom of the trunk. Don't throw it away. Don't tear it apart and rewrite it. Put it in another envelope and send it out to somebody else."

Persistence. As true as it is for any writer, it's especially true for the twenty-three-year writing career of McIntyre. For her, it began in high school.

"I got a little positive feedback for stories I wrote in high school, despite a 'creative writing' teacher who gave me a B because she made it a policy never to give an A to anyone the first time they were in her class. I took a couple of 'creative writing' classes in college, but found them useless to damaging. One instructor wanted everyone to write about 'real stuff,' like Hemingway: wars, bar-room brawls, drinking. That good everyday slice o' life stuff. Since we were all eighteen years old and eighteen year olds aren't even allowed in bars in Washington state, it was a pretty silly expectation."

So who did encourage her? "I did get positive feedback in college from friends, some of whom used to wait to read pages I was writing as they came out of the typewriter. I also got a good deal of encouragement from The Nameless Ones, the Seattle SF group that used to publish *Cry of the Nameless*. I wrote a column for its second incarnation, in the late 1960s. F. M. and Elinor Busby were the editors—they'd won a Hugo for the zine during its first incarnation. Then I attended the original Clarion workshop, which was a particularly encouraging incubator."

And her first big publishing break?

"As it happened, Andy Porter was the slush-pile reader for *The Magazine of Fantasy & Science Fiction*. He pulled my first story out of the slush-pile and gave it to Ed Ferman, the editor at the time. Ed didn't buy that story, but he wrote me a note about it, and he bought the next piece I sent him. I never did get the first story published, though it was accepted—after twenty-seven submissions. Fantasy editors said, 'I like this a lot, but it isn't fantasy, it's SF,' and SF editors said, 'I like this a lot, but it isn't SF, it's fantasy.' The editor who finally accepted it emigrated to New Zealand and neither he nor the manuscripts were ever heard from again, at least by me."

So of course she then entered an apprenticeship of the usual weird writer jobs. Right? Wrong.

"I was very lucky; I sold the second story I ever submitted, when I was twenty, sold several more during the following few months, and went to Clarion in the summer of 1970. The transition to full-time writing was intermittent rather than gradual. I've never had a real job, but for a while I made my living as an itinerant conference organizer—spotty employment. Some friends rented me a summer cabin for a low rent. I lived there on and off for several years. The cabin had a loft up in the eaves, so I suppose you could say I wrote part of *The Exile Waiting* and most of *Dreamsnake* in a garret. But it was an exceptionally pleasant garret. I dedicated *Exile* to the friends who rented me the place. The last conference I helped organize was in 1974—I was working on it when Nixon resigned. Joe Elder at Fawcett Gold Medal had bought *Exile*; 'Of Mist, and Grass, and Sand' had won the Nebula; Susan Rubinyi-Anderson and I were finishing up the original anthology *Aurora*."

Year after year, the books came. First was *The Exile Waiting* (Fawcett Gold Medal, 1975). Then *Dreamsnake* (Houghton Mifflin, 1978), *The Entropy Effect* (Timescape, 1981), *Superluminal* (Houghton Mifflin, 1983), and *Barbary* (Houghton Mifflin, 1986); the *Star Trek* movie novelizations *The Wrath of Khan* (Pocket, 1982), *The Search for Spock* (Pocket, 1984), *The Voyage Home* (Pocket, 1986) and the original SF novel *Enterprise: The First Adventure* (Pocket, 1986); the movie novelization *The Bride* (Dell, 1985); and more recently, the first 3 titles in the 4 book *Starfarers* series: *Starfarers* (Ace, 1989), *Transition* (Bantam, 1991), *Metaphase* (Bantam, 1992), with the fourth book—*Nautilus*—in progress. Her short stories were gathered in the collection *Fireflood & Other Stories* (Houghton Mifflin, 1976), while she co-edited with Ms. Rubinyi-Anderson the highly acclaimed *Aurora: Beyond Equality* (Fawcett Gold Medal, 1976), an anthology of humanist fiction containing stories by Ursula K. Le Guin, James Tiptree Jr., A.R. Sheldon, Marge Piercy, Dave Skal, P.J. Plauger and others.

Before choosing a writing career, she had graduated with a B.S. from the University of Washington, and earned about half a Ph.D. in genetics before she quit to write. Why did she choose writing over the life of a research scientist?

"As a research scientist, I make a very good SF writer. Seriously: scientific research requires a certain type of dogged patience, to sustain you between the 'Ah ha!' events, that I simply don't possess."

Some readers have noticed that McIntyre often writes about people who seek the ways to bind together different cultures, different political philosophies, and different ways of life. What attracts her to these thematic choices?

"I'd describe what I'm doing as observing characters who have great differences but mostly manage to get along without forcing each other to conform, and without killing each other. Which is the ultimate way of forcing someone to conform, of course. I think one of the biggest dangers to our survival is intolerance of differences, the weird drive so many people have to force others to agree. I wonder what they're so frightened of?"

She writes about such characters "partly because I'm a knee-jerk liberal, a card-carrying ACLU member, and partly because I am sick to death of SF in which military organizations—or organizations that claim not to be military, but walk like a duck, look like a duck, and quack like a duck . . . a duck in uniform—flood the galaxy. What utter nonsense. In the *Starfarers* series, I liked the idea of a 'bunch of disorganized anarchists'—as Griffith calls them—setting out to explore other star systems, with the intention of learning things and meeting people instead of conquering planets and proving human superiority. I liked the idea that everything wouldn't always go right, and that when things went wrong, nobody would leap into the engine room with a left-handed frammistat and save the day by contravening some basic law of physics. I wanted to write a science fiction novel that was a novel set in a conceivable, realistic future, rather than a novel that could as well be set in the present, except for a lot of bells and whistles."

What about writing from the point of view of a different gender? How successful does she think a writer can be doing that?

"How successful can a writer be who chooses to write only about a single gender? Whether I write from the point of view of a man or a woman, or write about men and women from the point of view of one character—of whichever gender—my job is to make individuals believable. This goes for characters of different cultural backgrounds, too. 1950's SF was mostly about young, single, well-educated white male loners. No matter who wrote it. Octavia Butler has some cogent things to say about how this affected her early writing. Fiction that restricted presents an awfully narrow world view."

Then do her interests extend into issues dealing with the Great Goddess, New Age themes, and what is sometimes called neo-paganism?

"Not being a religious person, I don't have any opinion on the subjects, except that—based on what little I know about them—they aren't any sillier than most 'mainstream' religions. I have a basic philosophical problem with any organization—religious, quasi-religious, pseudo-scientific, or secular—that exists mainly to separate people from large amounts of money. That's how I'd judge the various organizations, rather than by whether they were mainstream or New Age. And I suspect television evangelists would come out at the top of the curve on the score of separating people from their money."

She does, however, speak well of magic realism. "One of the best new voices in SF, Kathleen Alcalà, is a magic realist. I don't believe in magic *per se*; on the other hand, I think reality is magical in a lot of ways."

Her reading tastes include both SF and non-SF books, although "it's hard for me to read other SF while I'm working on a book of my own—which is usually. I'm not sure why. I like Le Guin, Delany, Zelazny, Varley. I wish Russ would write another novel. I like Wilhelm, Robin McKinley, Daniel M. Pinkwater, John Crowley. Many of the newer writers, such as Deborah Wessell ("The Cool Equations"), Eleanor Arnason (*A Woman of the Iron People*), and John Barnes (*Orbital Resonance*). I like mysteries for light reading, partly because it isn't as painful when a mystery is bad as when an SF novel disappoints me. I think Liza Cody is terrific, I enjoy Dick Francis, even when he's writing the same book over and over again and the bones of the research show through. I also like Marcia Muller, Sara Paretsky, and Aaron Elkins. It's awfully depressing what television did to Elkins' character Gideon Oliver, especially after getting my hopes up by taking the brilliant step of getting Lou Gossett Jr. to play him.

"Even if I don't have time to read all of *Natural History* when it arrives, I read Stephen Jay Gould's column. I enjoy it even when I don't agree with him. I read a good bit of non-fiction, but I'm more likely to choose it because of the subject than because of the author." And which writers have influenced her the most? "A difficult question; the answer probably changes depending on the phase of the moon. Delany and Le Guin, for various reasons."

The big question—does she intend to write more in the *Star Trek* universe? "It was fun to play in Gene Roddenberry's universe, but that's in my past. One should never say 'never' in this business, but the last time I wrote a *Star Trek* novel was in 1985." Well then, what about screenplays? And Hollywood.

"My entire experience with Hollywood, from on-spec scripts—that's the TV version of the slush-pile—for established series, to ideas solicited from me by a new SF television show, to an SF series that a network asked me to propose, has been the Hollywood 'No.' This consists of hysterical enthusiasm followed by endless silence. Almost no one in Hollywood has the nerve to say 'No' to your face, because they're afraid that next week you'll be their boss. And in Hollywood—Hollyweird, as its inhabitants call it—that can happen.

"I've never made a penny from TV or movie options on my work. But I've written a screenplay for *Dreamsnake* and I'm looking into independent production. So far, the return rate of my phone calls has been zero percent if the person I'm calling is in Hollywood, and one hundred percent if the person I'm calling is in the Northwest. Guess where I'll make the movie, when and if somebody hands me $15 million to do it with?"

Since she is not yet independently wealthy, I asked her about how she goes about the job of writing in her nice, older home in a suburb of Seattle. Does she use a computer and work in a separate study?

"I have an office. I compose in longhand and transfer the text onto a computer. I'm not so hidebound about this that I won't continue writing on the computer if the story keeps flowing after I'm done with the transcription. But I do find that I can type faster than I can think. When I compose on the computer, I always have to go back and cut out the extra words. Recast sentences that begin with 'There was,' for example. Until a couple of years ago I used a completely obsolete CPM Computer with eight-inch disk drives. Don't laugh. It was state of the art when I bought it. Obsolete computers are perfectly adequate for a writer. I got a new machine more out of a desire for some bells and whistles than for any absolute necessity. The bells and whistles can be dangerous—one of the signs of a novice, from an editor's point of view, is a submission that arrives looking typeset. Far from being the sign of a professional and a favor to the editor, that kind of manuscript is hard to read and much more difficult to put into production. The more a manuscript looks like it came out of a very good typewriter, the better. I went to some trouble and expense with my first computer to bully the printer into printing a typewriter-style manuscript. It was some time before computers could reliably produce copy that compares with a Selectric with a good Courier type ball and a carbon ribbon."

With that methodology, then, how long does it take her to finish a novel? And does she consider herself an instinctive or an analytical writer? "It takes me about a year to write a novel," she said.

"I'm always a little afraid to answer the question, 'How do you write a novel?' Some people will inevitably take the reply as a prescription for How To Write. All I can say is, if you're ever in a writing class where the instructor wants everybody to work the same way—generally, exactly the way the instructor works—your best move would be to run like hell. Everybody does this job differently. Whatever works for you is right.

"That said, the way I do it is to discover the story as I write it. I can't imagine being interested in a story that I'd had to outline in any detailed way. For example, Enterprise had a very tight deadline, because Paramount didn't decide to publish a 20th anniversary *Star Trek* novel till what amounts in publishing to the last minute. I set to work as soon as the editor said he liked my 'U.S.O. tour saves the galaxy' idea. Otherwise, the book wouldn't have been finished in time. When I was about half done, the editor gave me a call. He told me that Paramount liked the idea, but wanted a detailed outline before they'd approve it. I said, 'Look, they can have a detailed outline, or they can have a completed novel. They can't have both, and they have to pay me the same either way.' He laughed, and he must have read the riot act to Paramount, because I never heard another word about the detailed outline."

What kind of relationship does she like to have with an editor?

"Mutual respect."

What about advances—have hers been high?

"I think the more important—and more depressing—fact to know is that I sold my first novel twenty years ago for the exact same 'average' advance as an acquaintance sold a first novel for in 1993."

Does that mean she is concerned about the last ten years of corporate consolidation among book publishers? Yes.

"There are fewer places to submit your book. When the multinationals first started moving in, hopeful speculation had money flowing in to increase mid-list advances and support first novels, but this hasn't happened much as far as I can tell."

Then what advice does she have for new writers about the business of writing? "You have to want to be a writer, you can't just want to have written. You have to be persistent. It's a weird and chancy profession, and you have to pay both halves of your social-security tax."

McIntyre is also concerned about a writer's growth as a writer. "I think there's pressure on writers not to grow in certain ways. I've been quite fortunate with my novels, but every time I write a short story and try to sell it, I get responses such as 'Sure wish you'd sent us something just like the last story you published.' I'm always tempted to write back and say, 'I did send you the last story I published, and you rejected it, too,' but so far I've resisted that very bad idea. Besides, getting rejected when you've been in the business twenty years keeps you humble."

Despite rejections, she still enjoys the writing. "One of the things I like is the freedom to handle my own time. I'm like Travis McGee, John D. MacDonald's 'salvage expert,' who took his retirement a little at a time. Every so often I go off and do something strange that I wouldn't be able to do if I had to work nine-to-five, fifty weeks per year. But there are lots of things to dislike about writing. Sometimes you can't take off time, even if you're sick. For several books I met deadlines that if I'd had time to think about them, I would have said were impossible. Some of the drawbacks to writing are drawbacks for anyone who's self-employed. You get paid at long, sometimes irregular intervals and you often don't know how much you're going to be paid until the check arrives. Big companies think they need your money more than you do. You have to buy your own health insurance. That kind of thing."

She's modest when asked whether she feels she's matured as a stylist. "I think that's for other people to say. Besides, how do you measure style, in what units, and what's the baseline? When

I look back over my early work I think most of it is readable, but some is overwritten. These days I work on stripping prose down to its basics. I don't know how successful I am." She has been successful enough to win both a Hugo and a Nebula, and to garner additional Hugo and Nebula nominations for shorter pieces. Is that important to her? "It's very flattering to be recognized by both one's readers and one's professional colleagues."

In an equally serious vein, she's very concerned about present-day censorship efforts and the influence of special interest groups on libraries and publishers. "This is extremely scary. Censorship will never solve any of society's problems. It will only drive them underground and drain resources and energy into futile campaigns and away from efforts that might help the problems."

Discussions of censorship these days often co-occur with mention of the NEA. Does she think the U.S. should undertake greater funding of the arts and creative persons, as is done in Canada and Europe?

"I'm not opposed to the idea, but since I make a decent living on my own, I wouldn't feel particularly comfortable about taking government money myself. I did apply for an NEA grant once, many years ago, when I was young and foolish and poor. The rejection letter gave me the distinct impression that the judges were afraid of getting 'sci-fi' cooties. That experience may have colored my reaction just a bit.

"If government does fund the arts, I think the funding should go to younger and/or newer artists, dangerous art, experimental art, risky art, scary art. What's art for, if not shaking people up? And so what if once in a while someone gets a grant and produces crap? If you aren't allowed to fail, you can't take risks. If you know what's going to happen, it isn't an experiment."

Occasionally, she takes time out from writing to do a speaking gig or teach at a workshop. She's served as visiting novelist at Humboldt State University, worked for a Summer Arts program at California State University, spoken at Rutgers University on the "Implications of Genetic Engineering," and given other talks at Antioch West, the University of Washington, the Harbourfront International Author's Festival, and the Melbourne Writers Workshop. And she's done readings everywhere.

What does she do for fun? Besides writing?

"Reading, needlepoint, aikido, forestry. Various liberal and tree-hugger causes. When George Bush accused Michael Dukakis of being a card-carrying ACLU member, why didn't Dukakis whip out his ACLU card and say, 'You bet I am, George—you mean you aren't? What do you have against civil liberties?'"

Like her books and like her characters, Vonda N. McIntyre believes in engaging with life.

Fully. 𝒱

Photo by Betty Udesen, *The Seattle Times*.

Obituaries

Tom Whitmore
Vonda N. McIntyre, Official Obituary

AWARD-WINNING SEATTLE SCIENCE FICTION AUTHOR Vonda N. McIntyre died April 1, 2019, of pancreatic cancer. She was 70.

McIntyre wrote novels, short stories and media tie-in books, edited a ground-breaking anthology of feminist SF, and founded the Clarion West Writing Workshop. She won the Hugo, Nebula and Locus awards for her 1979 novel *Dreamsnake*, and won the Nebula again for her 1996 novel *The Moon and the Sun*. Her short stories were also nominated for awards. In media fiction, she will probably be most remembered as the author who gave Ensign Sulu a first name (Hikaru) in her *Star Trek* novel *The Entropy Effect*: that name was later written into one of the *Star Trek* films. With Susan Janice Rubinyi-Anderson, McIntyre edited one of the first feminist science fiction anthologies (*Aurora: Beyond Equality*, 1976). She was a participant in the Women in Science Fiction Symposium edited by Jeffrey D. Smith (*Khatru #3/4*, 1975—reprinted with additional material as by Jeanne Gomoll, lulu.com, 2008) with Chelsea Quinn Yarbro, Ursula K. Le Guin, Samuel R. Delany, James Tiptree Jr. and others. Her Nebula-winning fantasy novel *The Moon and the Sun* has been made into an as-yet-unreleased film, *The King's Daughter*, starring Pierce Brosnan. Much of the film was shot in Versailles, and McIntyre delighted in telling how kind Brosnan was to her when she visited the set.

McIntyre founded Book View Café, an online publishing collective for member authors to sell their e-books. When she developed some joint problems in her hands, she began making what she called "beaded sea creatures," which she regularly gave to friends and charity auctions. She had a lively correspondence with *Scientific American* columnist Martin Gardner about them, and some of them are in the Smithsonian Institution.

Vonda Neel McIntyre was born in Louisville, Kentucky, in 1948. Her family moved to Seattle in the early 1960s, and she earned a BS in biology from the University of Washington. She went on to graduate school in genetics at UW. In 1970, she attended the Clarion SF Writing Workshop—and in 1971, with the blessing of Clarion founder Robin Scott Wilson, she founded the Clarion West Writing Workshop in Seattle. McIntyre continued to be involved with the workshop throughout her life. She enjoyed a close friendship with Ursula K. Le Guin throughout her career that included various editing and publishing ventures.

The Seattle science fiction community recalls McIntyre as the "fairy godmother" to hundreds of Clarion West graduates, many of whom have gone on to be bright stars in the publishing world. "Vonda was one of Clarion West's founders, and has always been our fairy godmother, bringing comfort and whimsy to class after class with her impromptu visits and gifts of crocheted sea creatures," said novelist Nisi Shawl, a Clarion West board member. "She was the Good Witch of the Northwest, a fearless public reader and a stellar private writer who is missed by all."

A memorial service will be arranged in Seattle. McIntyre requested that, in lieu of flowers, people make memorial donations to one of their favorite charities.

Vonda N. McIntyre did ten times as much behind the scenes in the science fiction community than she did out in the open. Her award-winning stories, her media tie-ins, and her editing were all quite visible, and important: more important in the long run will be her legacy of support for individuals and institutions.

After going to the Clarion workshop in Pennsylvania, where she roomed next to Octavia E. Butler, she decided to found a similar workshop on the West Coast. With the aid of Clarion founder Robin Scott Wilson, she started (and ran for three years) Clarion West; when Marilyn Holt and J.T. Stewart decided to restart it in the 1980s, she continued to advise and support the workshop. Most of Clarion West's archives were stored in Vonda's basement. She was a regular donor of both money and items for their auctions.

She was the webmaster for SFWA for many years, and the webmaster for Book View Café as well.

She supported more writers than anyone realizes. Her friendship and support for Ursula K. Le Guin is well known: they published holiday cards together, and each regularly mentioned the other. She also was strong writing support for James Tiptree Jr., Paul Preuss, Molly Gloss, Nicola Griffith, Nisi Shawl, Octavia E. Butler, and just about anyone else who she met who wrote. She also listened to and cared for folks who didn't write. She was a quiet, tireless force helping bring women's voices forth in the SF community.

Her beaded sea creatures are almost pure Vonda. When she began to develop some pain in her hands from arthritis, she decided to take her crocheting skills and create beaded shapes reminiscent of nudibranchs and fractal patterns to give her the needed exercise to keep her hands supple. She began giving them to friends, donating them to charity auctions, and talking with people about them. She had a lively correspondence with Martin Gardner about them. The Smithsonian has examples of her work as well.

Vonda also helped out in small ways. Greg Bear commented about how happy Vonda was to wheel him around when he was temporarily in a wheelchair at the memorial for Karen K. Anderson, his mother-in-law. Every convention organizer who ever had her as a guest was pleased with her smile and her kindness to people working on the convention. She would not accept mistreatment, but never attacked. She had stories about all her friends, and would tell them whenever it was appropriate.

The SF community lost a major pillar today. *V*

Alan Boyle
Vonda N. McIntyre, 1948-2019:
Final Novel Adds to Seattle Science-fiction Star's Legacy

Originally published in *Geek Wire*, April 2, 2019

VONDA N. MCINTYRE, A LEADER of Seattle's science-fiction community who made her mark with *Star Trek* novels as well as the Clarion West Writers Workshop, has passed away at the age of 70.

McIntyre was diagnosed with pancreatic cancer eight weeks ago—but she managed to complete her final novel, titled *The Curve of the World*, less than two weeks before her death at home in Seattle on April 1.

"Be ready for a great read in a while!" her neighbor and friend Jane Hawkins reported in a posting to McIntyre's journal on the CaringBridge website.

The Kentucky native moved to Seattle with her family in the 1960s, and earned her bachelor's degree in biology from the University of Washington in 1970. In that same year, the young writer attended the Clarion Writers Workshop in State College, Pa. She was so impressed that she started up Clarion West in Seattle in 1971 while she was studying genetics in graduate school. That incarnation of the workshop lasted three years, but it was revived in Seattle by different organizers in the 1980s.

McIntyre won her first Nebula Award in 1973 for the novelette "Of Mist, and Grass, and Sand." That story was incorporated into her 1978 novel *Dreamsnake*, which won a Hugo award as well as another Nebula. *The Moon and the Sun* earned McIntyre her third Nebula in 1998. A movie based on that novel, *The King's Daughter* was filmed in 2014 and is awaiting theatrical release.

Her bibliography includes novelizations of *Star Trek II: The Wrath of Khan*, *Star Trek III: The Search for Spock* and *Star Trek IV: The Voyage Home*. She also wrote two other *Star Trek* books based on the original TV series, as well as a *Star Wars* novel and the *Starfarers* book series.

Starfarers grew out of a prank that McIntyre perpetrated during a science-fiction convention. Having been asked to speak on a panel about SF on TV—and realizing that it was likely to include another tired tirade about how awful it was—she planned ahead. During the panel, she said, "Wait a minute. I can't believe this. Haven't you people been watching the *Starfarers* miniseries?"

McIntyre said her detailed description left the audience convinced that they'd missed a badly scheduled and unadvertised miniseries. But the story underlying the non-existent show was so good that McIntyre decided she'd make it real in another way. That's how she came to write the four *Starfarers* novels.

McIntyre was a founding member of the Book View Cafe, an author-owned publishing cooperative, and was active in Science Fiction and Fantasy Writers of America. GeekWire contributor Frank Catalano said her passing was "very sad" on a personal level.

"She was a friend since I moved to Seattle in the early 1980s, a great help to me when I was overseeing the administration of the Nebula Awards and as a SFWA officer, and always a practical, humorous and calm voice of writing encouragement," Catalano said.

McIntyre's friends are planning a private memorial gathering within the next few days. A public reception will be scheduled within about a month, with details to be announced on the CaringBridge website. Her papers will be archived at the University of Oregon, which also preserves the literary papers of another well-known Pacific Northwest science-fiction writer, Ursula K. Le Guin. *V*

Marine flatworms by Vonda.

And In Her Own Words

Vonda N. McIntyre
I Will Walk with You

Originally posted in *Bookview Café*, April 15, 2015.

I'M DISTRESSED TO SEE that some folks who were planning to come to Sasquan are thinking of skipping Worldcon this year. Because they're frightened.

I understand why people are frightened, given the racist, misogynistic, and dishonest screeds they've been subjected to. It isn't—alas—unusual for verbal abuse to escalate into physical abuse; and anyway verbal abuse is no fun to begin with.

But I was thinking about what might help counterbalance the situation.

Have you seen news reports of people responding to threats against a particular group by offering "I'll ride with you"? Here's the first Google hit off that phrase:

http://www.bbc.com/news/blogs-trending-30479306

I will walk with you at Worldcon.

I'm not very fond of confrontation. I'm a courtesy 5'1" and my 67th birthday (how did *that* happen?!) is just after the convention and I'm walking with a hiking pole while recovering from a hiking fall, an injury that's taking way longer to heal than when I was a pup.

On the other hand I'm a *shodan* in Aikido.

On the third hand, which I can have because I'm an SF writer, *shodan*—first degree black belt—is when you realize how much you still have to learn.

But I'm thinking that maybe it would make folks who feel threatened feel a little safer to have someone at their side, maybe even someone with a bunch o' fancy ribbons fluttering from her name badge, even if that person is shorter, smaller, and older than they are, white-haired and not physically prepossessing. It's another person's presence.

It might cause some abuse *not* to happen.

That would be the perfect Aiki solution.

Have I thought of the many ways this could go wrong? Or be subject to abuse?

For sure I have.

Have I figured out how to organize and manage this offer?

Not so much, yet, but I'm working on it.

Am I restricting this offer to members of one "side" or the other? No.

Everyone pretty much knows that I'm of the tree-hugging, knee-jerk liberal, feminist stripe. But if you are a Puppy, and you're frightened, the offer holds for you, too. I may choose not to converse with you (you know why; I don't like verbal abuse any more than anybody else), but I will walk with you.

This is not a Sasquan event. The con committee members have plenty on their plate already.

I make the offer in good faith. Whoever you are: If you would feel more comfortable walking with me from a program item to another program item, to the con suite, to your room, when my schedule allows, I'll walk with you.

I probably will decline to enter your hotel room to scare off the monsters under the bed, but I'll do my best to make sure you get safely to where you're going, free of monsters. 𝒱

Jack Skillingstead, Nancy Kress and Vonda. Photo provided by Nancy Kress.

Vonda N. McIntyre
The Story of Why Vonda Wrote Starfarers

Originally posted on mybookthemovieblogspot.com, December 23, 2009

STARFARERS DIDN'T START OUT AS A NOVEL QUARTET. It didn't start out as a single novel, a short story, or prose. It started out as a hoax.

Some years back, I was to be on a SF convention panel, "Science Fiction on Television." This panel used to turn up at conventions with some regularity, and it always followed the same pattern: somebody pulled out a list of all the SF television series of the recent past and read it aloud, inviting the audience to agree how terrible all the shows were. (Since then, things have changed, and some good SF has been on TV, but at that time aside from *Twilight Zone* and the original *Star Trek*, you had choices such as *Time Tunnel* and *Lost in Space*.)

This particular panel bores me to death, so, having promised to be on it, I had to do something different.

I had always thought the TV miniseries was the perfect form for SF—I wished *Masterpiece Theater* would produce one of our field's classics—but at the time no one had tried it.

When the panelist next to me whipped out his list and started to read titles, to the audience's groans, I let him get through a couple of lines before I raised an eyebrow.

"Hold on," I said. "Haven't you seen *Starfarers*? Hasn't *anybody* seen *Starfarers*?"

Of course nobody had (because I made it up).

"It was a terrific miniseries. It was hard to find because CBS kept moving it around—isn't that always what happens with good shows? It was about an O'Neill colony starship, a university town in space, preparing for its first research expedition. But there's a political change, and the current administration decides the expedition should be canceled and the starship turned into an orbiting spy station.

"So the faculty and staff of the starship do what any red-blooded space explorers would do.

"They steal the starship."

I told the audience a little about the exploratory company:

J.D. Sauvage, alien contact specialist and long-distance swimmer, joining the alien contact team after a sojourn with a pod of killer whales and their genetically engineered human cousins, the divers (who live in Canada because they're technically at war with the USA);

Victoria Fraser MacKenzie, Canadian physicist, inventor of the starship's propulsion system, descendant of slaves who escaped via the Underground Railroad before the American Civil War;

Satoshi Lono, geographer, web-savvy night-owl and Marathon runner; *Stephen Thomas Gregory,* geneticist, oversupplied with good looks and charm that mask his troubled family past.

Victoria, Satoshi, and Stephen Thomas are members of a family partnership, trying to recover from the loss of their fourth partner, Merit.

The story was part space adventure, part alien contact story, part family saga.

At the end of the panel, local filmmaker Ryan Johnson was about to set out on a quest for videotapes of the series. I had to confess that the series was a hoax, "the best SF TV series never made." After a moment of disappointment, he said, "I'll make you a trailer!"

And he did.

Several friends formed the Starfarers Fan Club, and we did a number of panels at SF conventions over the next couple of years. I fondly remember one in which the next panel was "Hollywood screenwriting," and the panelists in the back of the room waiting for their panel to start were completely fooled by Ryan's trailer, which was designed to look like it had been fortuitously snagged off a TV broadcast.

We always called *Starfarers* "the best SF TV series never made," and the audience almost always failed to hear the "never made" part.

After a few panels, I realized it was a pretty good story and I wanted to write it, so I did. It ended up being a quartet, which I think of as one long novel that I couldn't afford to write all at once: *Starfarers*, *Transition*, *Metaphase*, and *Nautilus*.

Over on the Book View Café blog, we were discussing casting possibilities, and the interesting idea came up of a vintage cast from 1940s movies. We kicked that around for a while.

It turned out to be impossible.

The problem with a vintage cast is that the faculty and staff of *Starfarer* is a diverse group. Satoshi is of Hawaiian and Japanese background, Victoria is Canadian. Stephen Thomas' boss is the daughter of Cambodian refugees. J.D. has six biological and social parents, and Zev is from a family that has chosen genetic engineering to allow them to live in the sea. Stephen Thomas is one of the few people in the book who's the default human being as far as movies are concerned: a white guy in his late twenties or early thirties. And even he isn't quite "default," not that you can tell by looking, because like most of the characters in *Starfarers*, Stephen Thomas chooses his lovers for other qualities than whether they're of the opposite sex. One hopes that if a series were made of *Starfarers*, the producers would honor the diversity of the people in it, and not claim (as happens far too often) that because they were color-blind with casting, it really wasn't important or significant that everybody turned out to be white. That claim is just plain ridiculous.

Aside from a diverse cast of human characters, the quartet includes biomechanical creatures (the silver slugs and the artificial stupids) and aliens who are alien physically as well as culturally. None of the aliens is remotely human. One group vaguely resembles six-limbed meerkats. One being is the size of an island, and another is as delicate and insubstantial as vacuum.

And then there is Nemo, the squidmoth.

As J.D. thinks, at the end of *Transition*: *Squidmoths?*

Those folks are going to require some serious CGI.

So who *would* be my ideal (human, or mostly human) cast? When I wrote the novels and when we were doing the Starfarers panels, we had a cast in mind, but some of the actors are no longer in the business. The vintage cast was a no-go, and while it was tempting to try for a time-travelling 1960s cast (mainly because Peter O'Toole in his *Lawrence of Arabia* days would have been perfect as Stephen Thomas, and Peter O'Toole is in all my favorite movies, and *Lawrence of Arabia* is my candidate for the best movie ever made), I decided to go with contemporary actors.

Alien Contact Specialist J.D. Sauvage is Camryn Manheim. She can be funny or serious, sexy or reserved. You can believe her as a long-distance swimmer and as a person who could make friends even with alien intelligences.

For Victoria Fraser MacKenzie, I want Tracy Heggins. Heggins would be perfect for the sophisticated and politically savvy head of the Alien Contact Team. Victoria is a physicist, but she's no girl geek. Heggins is stunning; she projects intelligence and strength. She can also be vulnerable—an important quality for Victoria, who is still grieving over the loss of the fourth member of her family partnership, Merit.

For Stephen Thomas Gregory: Cillian Murphy. Stephen Thomas is the biologist of the team, preternaturally handsome, very smart, the newest partner and youngest of the family, the person knocked most off-center by the death of Merit, who proposed to him.

And for Satoshi Lono, the geographer of the Alien Contact Team, and the person whose good sense, intelligence, passion, and love keeps the family partnership from dissolving?

George Takei, of course.

There may be some truth to the suggestion that the *Starfarers* group developed Satoshi for Takei,to give him a part to play where he got to do a good deal more than navigate a starship. And if Satoshi is some years older than the rest of the Alien Contact Team, older than the other members of the family partnership?

That's OK.

George Takei is timeless. 𝒱

Vonda, May 2006, WisCon 30. Photo by Mike Ward.

Early Years, Family

Vonda and Carolyn McIntyre. Provided by Stacey Vilas.

Vonda (left) and Carolyn (right), with their mother, Vonda (Keith) McIntyre. Photo provided by Stacey Vilas.

Thanksgiving with Vonda (left) and Carolyn (right) and their parents, H. Neel McIntyre, and Vonda (Keith) McIntyre. Photo provided by Stacey Vilas.

Carolyn and Vonda with their mother, Vonda (Keith) McIntyre. Photo provided by Stacey Vilas.

Vonda in a tree. Photo from Vonda's files.

Vonda. Photo provided by Stacey Vilas.

Vonda (on horseback) and Carolyn with their mother, Vonda (Keith) McIntyre. Photo provided by Stacey Vilas.

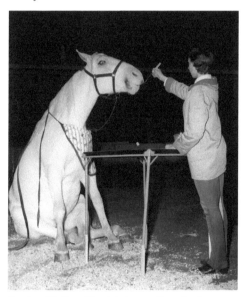

Vonda with Mom Vonda's horse, Snowfy—known by Vonda and Carolyn as the best horse in the world. Photo by Dick Harris.

(from left to right) Carolyn, Mom Vonda, Vonda on Snowfy, and father, H. Neel McIntyre. Photo provided by Stacey Vilas.

Sisters, Carolyn and Vonda, 2014. Photo by Stacey Vilas.

Vonda and her sister Carolyn, 2018, at Duckabush. Photo by Stacey Vilas.

Bibliography

Novels

The Curve of the World, Handheld Press, pending.

The Exile Waiting (reprint) Handheld Press, pending Fall, 2019

The Moon and the Sun. Pocket Books, September 1997. Nebula Award, 1998. Book View Café e-book, September 2008.

The Starfarers Series:

Starfarers. Easton Press; Ace Books, 1989, ISBN 9780441780532; Bantam Spectra, 1994, ISBN 978-0-553-56341-2.

Transition. Easton Press; Bantam Books, 1991; Bantam Spectra 1994.

Metaphase. Bantam Spectra, 1992, 1994.

Nautilus. Bantam Spectra, 1994.

Barbary, Houghton Mifflin, 1986; Berkley, 1988. (For younger readers.)

Superluminal. Houghton Mifflin; Pocket Books, 1984. Book View Café ebook, forthcoming.

Dreamsnake. Houghton Mifflin, 1978; Dell, 1979, Bantam Spectra 1994. Hugo, Nebula, Locus, Pacific Northwest Booksellers Association awards. Book View Café ebook, 26 April 2009.

The Exile Waiting. SF Book Club, 1975; Fawcett Gold Medal, 1975; Victor Gollancz, 1976; Tor, 1985.

Star Trek Novels

The Entropy Effect. Timescape, 1981 (original Star Trek novel #1).

Star Trek II: The Wrath of Khan. Pocket Books, 1982 (based on the movie script).

Star Trek III: The Search for Spock, Pocket Books, 1984 (based on the movie script).

Star Trek IV: The Voyage Home, Pocket Books, 1986 (based on the movie script).

Enterprise: The First Adventure, Pocket, 1986 (original Star Trek "giant" novel #1 for the 20th anniversary).

Other Tie-in Novels

Star Wars: The Crystal Star, Bantam Spectra, 1994.

The Bride, Dell Books, 1985 (based on the movie script for a remake of *The Bride of Frankenstein*).

Short Story Collection

Fireflood and Other Stories. Houghton Mifflin, Pocket Books, 1979.

"Fireflood," *The Magazine of Fantasy & Science Fiction.* November 1979.

"Of Mist, and Grass, and Sand," *Analog.* October 1973. Nebula award.

"Spectra," *Orbit 11,* ed. Damon Knight. G.P. Putnam, 1972.

"Wings," *The Alien Condition*, ed. Stephen Goldin. Ballantine, 1973.

"The Mountains of Sunset, the Mountains of Dawn." *The Magazine of Fantasy & Science Fiction*, February 1974. *The Norton Book of Science Fiction*, ed. Le Guin, Attebery, Fowler, 1993.

"The End's Beginning," *Analog*, September 1976.

"Screwtop," *The Crystal Ship*, ed. Marta Randall. Nelson 1976.

"Only at Night," *Clarion*, ed. Robin Scott Wilson. Signet 1971.

"Recourse, Inc.," *Alternities*, ed. David Gerrold. Dell 1974.

"The Genius Freaks," *Orbit 12*, ed. Damon Knight. G.P. Putnam, 1973.

"Aztecs," *2076: The American Tricentennial*, ed. Edward Bryant. Pyramid 1977. Nebula nomination, 1977.

Uncollected Short Stories

"LADeDeDa," by Ursula K. Le Guin & Vonda N. McIntyre. *Nature* "Futures," 12 March 2009.

"The Natural History and Extinction of the People of the Sea," a Book View Café Bonus, 16 November 2008. Illustrated by Ursula K. Le Guin.

"Misprint," *Nature* 454, 252–252. Futures. 9 Jul 2008.

"A Modest Proposal for the Perfection of Nature," *Nature* 434, p. 122. Futures. 3 Mar 2005. Reprint: *Futures from Nature*, ed. Henry Gee, Tor, November 2007; *Year's Best* SF 11, ed. Hartwell & Cramer, June 2006.

"Little Faces," *SciFiction*, ed. Ellen Datlow. February 2006. Nebula nomination, 2007.

"Night Harvest," *Odyssey* #4, ed. Liz Holliday, 1998. Book View Café, November 2008.

"The Adventure of the Field Theorems," *Sherlock Holmes in Orbit*, ed. Mike Resnick & Martin H. Greenberg. DAW 1995.

"Steelcollar Worker," *Analog*, November 1992.

"Malheur Maar," *Full Spectrum* 2, ed. Lou Aronica, Shawna McCarthy, Amy Stout, & Pat Lobrutto; Doubleday 1989.

"Elfleda," *New Dimensions 12*, ed. Marta Randall & Robert Silverberg. Pocket Books, 1981.

"Looking for Satan," *Shadows of Sanctuary*, ed. Robert Lynn Asprin and Lynn Abbey; Ace 1981.

"Shadows, Moving," *Interfaces*, ed. Ursula K. Le Guin & Virginia Kidd. Ace 1980.

"Thanatos," *Future Power*, ed. Jack Dann & Gardner Dozois. Random House 1976.

"The Galactic Clock," *Generation*, ed. David Gerrold. Dell 1972.

"Cages," *Quark* 4, ed. Samuel R. Delany & Marilyn Hacker. Paperback Library 1971.

Essays

"Ursula K. Le Guin: Mutinous Navigator"

"Frank Herbert Memorial Sunset Watch"

"The Straining Your Eyes Through the Viewscreen Blues," *Nebula Winners 15* (1981)

Poetry

"Diamond Craters," *Newsletter of the Alabama Geological Society*, Spring 1993.

Anthologies

Nebula Awards Showcase 2004, ed. Vonda N. McIntyre. Roc Trade, March 2004. ISBN-10: 0451459571. ISBN-13: 978-0451459572

Aurora: Beyond Equality, Fawcett Gold Medal, 1976, edited by Vonda N. McIntyre & Susan Janice Anderson, editors

Podcasts, Audiobooks, & Audio Downloads

"A Modest Proposal for the Perfection of Nature," Starship Sofa, Aural Delights #33, narrated by Amy H. Sturgis. 19 July 2008. Direct link to MP3

The Moon and the Sun: Audible.com audio download; Blackstone Audiobooks Cassette, CD, MP3CD. Unabridged. Read by Anna Fields.

Dreamsnake: Audible.com audio download; Blackstone Audiobooks Cassette, CD, MP3CD. Unabridged. Read by Anna Fields.

Contributors Index

A
Alma Alexander: 76
K.G. Anderson: 47
Tanya Avakian: 46

B
Harriet Beeman: 118
Gary L. Benson: 81
Rhonda Boothe: 30
Alan Boyle: 192

C
Liz Carey: 82
Amy Sterling Casil: 56
Lyman Caswell: 4
Frank Catalano: 82
Darrah Chavey: 34
Eli Cohen: 82
Frances Collin: 83
Julie E. Coryell: 68, 69
Brian Cronin: 48
Ctein: 70
Arwen Curry: 14

D
Jack Dann: 85
Doctor Science: 86
L. Timmel Duchamp: 32

E
Ellen Eades: 86
Laurie Toby Edison: 103
Anthony Evans: 86

F
Eric R. Franklin: 50
Gregory Frost: 61

G
Deb Geisler: 86
Glenn Glazer: 87
Molly Gloss: 15
Jeanne Gomoll: 23, 28, 33, 37, 132
William Grabowski: 87
Neile Graham: 17
Sarah Grant: 51
Susan Gray: 87
Eileen Gunn: 88

H
Ian K. Hagemann: 40
Donna Haraway: 71
Dick Harris: 209
Jane Hawkins: 122
Nina Kiriki Hoffman: 54
Marilyn Holt: 5
Leslie Howle: 66, 92

I
Jenny Islander: 226

J
JLH: 91
Lynn Johanna a.k.a. Lady Willow: 73

K
T. Jackson King: 173
Jay Kay Klein: 8
Nancy Kress: 91, 96, 198
Kevin Kuenkler: 95
Ole Kvern: 52

L
Mary Langenfeld: 36, 79
Fonda Lee: 90
Ursula K. Le Guin: 19
Alice Lengers: 106
John Lorentz: 95

M
Kate MacDonald: 97
Diane Martin: 39
Vonda N. McIntyre: 196, 199
Sean McNamara: 43, 110
Beth Meacham: 142
Nancy Jane Moore: 64

N
Sharan Newman: 100
Debbie Notkin: 103
Paul Novitski: 144

P
Shannon Page: 126, 129
Karen Dawn Plaskon: 72
Andrew Porter: 31
Paul Preuss: 101
Mary Prince: 34

R
Cat Rambo: 107
Neil Rest: 107
Robert Reynolds: 108
Candace Robb: 108
Jennifer Roberson: 109
Robyn: 108
Deborah Ross: 62
Susan Rubinyi-Anderson: 41
Carol Ryles: 109
Geoff Ryman: 109

S
Pamela Sargent: 111
Kate Schaefer: 14, 119
Nisi Shawl: 122
Sylvi Shayl: 126
Don Simmons: 4
Jon Singer: 128
Bret Smith: 130
Stephanie A. Smith: 24, 72, 131, 132
Pam Smith: 130
Sara Stamey: 133

T
Sheree Renée Thomas: 133

U
Betty Udesen: 186

V
Stacey Vilas: 121, 135, 206, 207, 208, 209, 210, 211
Tamara Vining: 133
Elisabeth Vonarburg: 100

W
Donna J. Wagner: 133
John Walters: 9
Cynthia Ward: 134
Mike Ward: 204
Graham Watt: 137, 138
Tom Whitmore: 136, 188
Eric Williams: 139
Chris Willrich: 139
Amy Wolf: 60, 140, 141

Y
Sara Yake: 142
Ygor and Buntho: 27

Z
Jill Zeller: 7

About this Book

JANE HAWKINS HAD AN IDEA: to collect all the lovely stories written around Vonda's death, and to put them in one place for us all to enjoy. This is that place. Stephanie A. Smith and Jeanne Gomoll joined forces to edit the book. Vonda's community—her friends, colleagues, readers, and admirers—shared their fondest memories, stories, praise and love for the dear friend they had recently lost.

All proceeds from this book will benefit Clarion West.

For helping to track down people, information and photos, we thank Frances Collin, Darrah Chavey, Ginger Clark, Marnee Chua, Mel Gilden, Mike Glyer, Jane Hawkins, Joe Manfredini, Andrew Porter, Kate Schaefer, Stacey Vilas, and Amy Wolf.

For proofreading assistance we thank: Debbie Notkin, Kate Schaefer, Tamara Vining, and Tom Whitmore.

Jeanne Gomoll designed and typeset the pages and designed the cover art. The text type is Adobe Jenson Pro, with titles in Mission Gothic, a font designed by James T. Edmondson. 𝒱